D0252679

The Way of Mindful Education

NORTON BOOKS IN EDUCATION

THE WAY OF MINDFUL EDUCATION

Cultivating Well-Being in Teachers and Students

DANIEL J. RECHTSCHAFFEN

Foreword by Jon Kabat-Zinn

W. W. Norton & Company
New York • London

The material on "Mindful Schools Lessons on Thoughts" found on page 277–287, including the exercises "Past/Present/Future," "First Thought," "Wrap up," as well as various journal/drawing questions and a description of the Mindful Schools organization is used courtesy of Mindful Schools, Inc. Learn more at www.mindfulschools.org.

For information about permission to reproduce selections from this book, write to Permissions, W. W. Norton & Company, Inc., 500 Fifth Avenue, New York, NY 10110

For information about special discounts for bulk purchases, please contact W. W. Norton Special Sales at specialsales@wwnorton.com or 800-233-4830

Manufacturing by Quad Fairfield
Production manager: Leeann Graham

ISBN: 978-0-393-70895-0

W. W. Norton & Company, Inc., 500 Fifth Avenue, New York, N.Y. 10110
www.wwnorton.com

W. W. Norton & Company Ltd., Castle House, 75/76 Wells Street, London W1T 3QT

1 2 3 4 5 6 7 8 9 0

This book is dedicated to my mother and father,
Stephan Rechtschaffen and Elizabeth Lesser,
for your unconditional love as parents,
for the wisdom you embody as individuals, and now
the honor of holding you as my friends.

CONTENTS

ACKNOWLEDGMENTS

This book is dedicated to all of my teachers and all of my students. Particularly to one student in an Oakland public school who gave me an orange crayon on my first day of teaching, so many years ago, and said, "This crayon means you're my best friend." That crayon still stands on my desk.

Thanks go to Martin Prechtel, for reminding me again and again to be reverent of the wisdom of our natural world, to listen ever more deeply, to sing ever more beautifully, to become a person worth descending from. To Thich Nhat Hahn, who taught me the art of walking, breathing, and smiling. To Jon and Myla Kabat-Zinn, who have so generously supported me in my work as they have for so many in this mindfulness movement. To my mentors and friends in the mindfulness in education community, especially Linda Lantieri, Susan Kaiser-Greenland, Daniel Siegel, the Mindful Education Institute family, and so many teachers and researchers who are dedicated to this common vision. Laurie Grossman and Richard Shankman, thank you for opening the doors to the Mindful Schools classrooms where I first learned the art of teaching mindfulness to kids. My psychology mentors, Mordechai Mitnick, Jennifer Welwod, Lucanna Grey, Jonathen Tenny, and Michael Kahn, opened my heart and taught me to be an authentic human being.

Thanks also to Caroline Pincus, for tinkering around with

me in the early iterations of the book that this has become. To Willow Ruth, for your eloquent editing and sweet friendship. To Nan Satter, for truly understanding this book and for the constructive craft of your words. To Deborah Malmud, for dispelling all of my negative myths about publishers. Your attentiveness, dedication, and kindness have breathed life into this book. To Benjamin Yarling for amazing me with your depth of understanding and insight into this book. Your brilliant edits have spiced every page. To the whole W. W. Norton team, thank you for your dedication to this material and your beautiful professionalism.

I thank my friend and writing compatriot, David Coates, for your insights and friendship that have helped me become the person I needed to be to write this book. To David Treleaven, Max Tarcher, the Essex crew, and everyone else who has read, listened, and supported me in this process.

And to my wife, my partner, my teacher, my friend, Taylor Pattinson. We met at midnight on New Year's Eve and talked in the darkness about mindfulness and education. Your enthusiasm then and your insightful wisdom every day since have been the fuel that has carried me through this journey. Nothing gives me more joy than the possibility of learning the true art of mindful education as we embark down the road of creating a family together.

FOREWORD

My first experience with Daniel Rechtschaffen's work was sitting in on a session he conducted in a middle school class in the Oakland Unified School District when he was working with a group known as Mindful Schools. This school had a reputation as one of the more challenging in the district. When I walked in, a bit late, the class of about twenty-five students was already in total silence. The atmosphere was utterly calm and attentive. Almost everybody was sitting up in his or her seat, but there was no sense of rigidity or stiffness. The students looked at home, and I immediately felt at home in the stillness and silence. I could hardly believe that middle school students were capable of it. The classroom teacher was sitting at the back of the room and Daniel was on a chair at the front. He was holding up a brass bowl. Slowly, as I took my seat at the back of the room, I saw hands being raised, a few to begin with, then more and more of them, all in silence. What was this? What was going on here? What was I observing? I had never seen anything like it before.

Well, it turned out that the instruction for this exercise was for the students to raise their hand when they could no longer hear the sound of the bell. Daniel had struck the bowl with a stick right before I walked in. Apparently listening for the absence of something invited tremendous attending, even among middle school students.

That same day, I visited an elementary school in the same district and saw another mindfulness instructor from Mindful Schools do the same exercise with first graders, again, with the teacher at the back of the room and the instructor at the front. After inviting the children to "put on their mindfulness bodies"—at which point the children all sat up erect in their seats and got very still—and without saying anything more, she rang the bowl in the same way Daniel had. Again, the sound reverberated through the room and slowly, as it receded, I saw little hands being raised, one-by-one, all in silence. The longer it went, the more hands were raised.

This first-grade teacher later shared with me that many of the children in her class had serious attentional problems. She was astonished at how still the room became during these sessions. It was a skill that over time, she found transferred to other moments in the day when she could invite the class to settle, since they knew what it felt like, making it easier to teach the subject curriculum (1).

Primary and secondary school teachers are becoming increasingly pressured to be even more outwardly focused, driven by the "teaching to the test" directive and culture that so dominates education at this time. The overwhelming emphasis is on information and facts, with the laudable aim, of course, of engendering greater knowledge and understanding in the next generation, and thereby, an educated and presumably maximally creative and effective workforce for the world of the future. Except that the approach itself may be sorely lacking and misguided, perhaps effective for a minority of students, but leaving the majority behind; increasingly stressed, alienated, terminally bored, and even turned off to learning. We could say that the dominant culture in K-12 education is creating a public health crisis in the sense that the health of the next generation depends crucially on skills and competencies that until recently were not the province of school at all.

Overlooked or ignored in the current atmosphere is the domain of interiority—of the inner life of the growing learner—and how it can and needs to be recognized, attended to, nurtured, and developed in concert with all the outer knowledge and competencies so that each child learns how to be at home in his or her own skin, how to calm his or her own mind and body, and how to cultivate self-awareness, emotional intelligence, confidence, and resilience in the face of stress of all kinds and the pressures to perform, to be a certain way, and to fit in. In my experience, nurturing and validating interiority also serves as a catalyst for creativity and imagination.

In the face of this consistent exclusion of the inner life of their students from the curriculum, more and more teachers are turning to mindfulness as a way to promote and support qualities such as the sense of agency, of being your own person, of being fundamentally OK as you are, of being whole, of belonging, in addition to developing specific competencies that are important in sustaining that wholeness over the years, and in optimizing learning. Such competencies include developing the ability to know and recognize our own thoughts and emotions as "events " in the field of awareness and how to disentangle ourselves when we are completely caught up in their content and emotional charge. Simple mindfulness practices can offer reliable strategies for working with the storms and turbulence that inevitably overtake the mind at times and cause sadness or anger, or a sense of not fitting in, of not being good enough, or even not wanting to learn. It promotes increased calmness, focus and concentration, greater impulse control and reduced aggression, and increased empathy and understanding of others among other important outcomes (2).

In making such practices an intimate and seamless part of the classroom experience—as described so effectively in this book—children are given practical opportunities to get to know and explore the terrain of their own being. This includes not only thoughts and emotions but also an awareness of the universe of body sensations, including one's own breathing, and how they are continually changing, often in concert with one's thoughts and emotions. Going further, it also includes social awareness, the landscape of being in relationship with others, and learning how to navigate that territory in satisfying ways that foster connection, kindness, and a range of pro-social behaviors rather than separation, disregard, and enmity.

Interiority and self-awareness require education and cultivation in parallel with the more academic curriculum for these competencies to take root, blossom, and continue to develop and deepen across the lifespan. That cultivation begins with exploring how to be still and what that feels like, how to move intentionally and what that feels like, and how to be maximally present whenever you choose to be or need to be. Mindfulness lies at the heart of social emotional learning. It is essentially about choosing wiser and more adaptive ways to be in relationship to one's inner and outer experience as it is unfolding moment by moment. As we will see, mindfulness adds an embodied practice element to SEL that is likely to help a child's responses be much more balanced, appropriate, and effective in moments of crisis or conflict.

At the heart of the cultivation of mindfulness is awareness itself. Awareness is not something we get or develop but rather something we discover we already have, a capacity that is innate but easily ignored in favor of thinking, another wonderful human capacity. But while thinking gets a lot of air time in school, with the hope of training students to be better and more critical thinkers, there is little or no attention paid to this other equally essential capacity of ours that can help modulate our thoughts and emotions and expand their range. The calling of these times is to discover and familiarize ourselves with this innate capacity and then learn to inhabit it, integrate it into our day, and make use of it in navigating the ins and outs and twists and turns of our unfolding lives. What better place to begin to tap into and nurture this dimension of intelligence than in school?

The cardinal quality of awareness is that it can contain anything and everything that arises in our experience with clarity and discernment and without immediately judging it—a suspension of the usual impulse to immediately categorize and evaluate every aspect of our experience in terms of liking and disliking it, or wanting more or wanting less. Awareness amplifies what is most human in us and expands our relationship with life itself and our responses to it. I think of it as perhaps the ultimate intrinsic characteristic of what makes us fully human.

The direct path to awareness and its intrinsic clarity is the systematic cultivation of attention. The virtues of introducing its cultivation and practice to school children are compelling.

Such skills and practices and the potential insights and under-standings that can arise from them are, to my mind, no longer optional in the human repertoire. They are absolutely essential for adults as well as children in our rapidly changing and increasingly complex, and often bewildering world, in which, as Linda Stone, a former Microsoft researcher put it, our "default mode" is increasingly one of *continuous partial attention* (3). They compliment the standard learning curriculum and make it easier to teach, as the Oakland first-grade teacher observed. They also don't take up a lot of time, especially in the hands of experienced teachers well-trained in mindfulness.

As this book skillfully documents, it is now well known that stress has deleterious effects on the developing brain (4). In particular, stress has been shown to degrade the executive functions of the prefrontal cortex—which is essential for prob-lem-solving, creativity, and reasoning—as well as the activity of the hippocampus, which plays an active and important role in learning, memory, and emotion regulation. Stress also affects the amygdalae, the threat reactivity centers within the brain's limbic system, which get bigger with ongoing stress exposure, and smaller with mindfulness training. For this reason alone, it makes sense to adopt and utilize simple attentional practices that we know through scientific studies can counter the toxic-ity of stress. Many children don't even come to school in a con-dition that would allow for learning. They may not have had breakfast that morning, or may have already experienced stress or even violence. Before they can teach the required curriculum, teachers are feeling the need to give their students the tools for self-regulation, for paying attention, for learning how to learn, for tuning their instrument (of learning) before attempting to play it, just as musicians tune their instruments before playing them. The practices in this book, if integrated into the lessons of the day, can help to buffer the deleterious effects of stress on the developing brains of the students. This is especially important for those children at highest risk and where the societal costs of failure to learn and thrive are most extreme.

Other studies over the past twenty years have demonstrated a dramatic decline in children in many of the cognitive and emotional competencies that we take for granted as the foundation for eventually becoming fully embodied adults and contributors to society (5). More recently, studies have revealed the importance of developing skills for deep listening and effective communication, conflict resolution, critical thinking, goal setting, and teamwork in public education (6). All these can be improved through mindfulness practice.

According to Linda Lantieri (7), a pioneering educator in Social Emotional Learning (SEL) and mindfulness, the added value that mindfulness brings to conventional SEL is primarily in the area of its *embodied practices*, known to promote neuroplasticity; that is, structural changes in the brain regions we just mentioned, as well as others, which have the potential to improve learning and memory, emotional balance, and cognitive perspective taking. Mindfulness practices put a solid experiential foundation underneath the more conceptually and cognitively-based SEL curriculum. They allow each child to regularly exercise the muscle of emotional balance through *practicing* being present and cultivating moment-to-moment non-judgmental awareness (my operational definition of mindfulness) in moments of relative calm, and then, over time, learning to maintain or recover a degree of equilibrium, even equanimity, in the face of stressful triggers and threats. The muscle of mindfulness, when exercised regularly, especially if it is done playfully and with a light touch, makes it more likely that the children will be able to call on and make use of their SEL strategies under threatening and highly emotional conditions.

My first introduction to mindfulness in the classroom came from a fifth grade public school teacher, the late Cherry Hamrick, at the Welby Elementary School in South Jordan, Utah in the early 1990s. Cherry was an intrepid and highly creative early pioneer in this movement (8). She decided to try to bring mindfulness into her classroom after participating in a Mindfulness-Based Stress Reduction (MBSR) program at the LDS Hospital in Salt Lake City. In spite of my initial skepticism, Cherry's introduction of mindfulness into her fifth grade curriculum in a number of creative ways was a very successful experiment that stretched out over a number of years. I had the privilege of visiting the school and meeting with her students and some of their parents. Mindfulness was obviously welcomed and having a positive impact not only in her classroom, but in the school more broadly during those years. One anecdote I vividly remember from that time: one of Cherry's fifth graders was overheard (by a parent) saying to one of her siblings when he was complaining about being teased by a classmate: "Just because his mind is waving doesn't mean that your mind has to wave."

Mindfulness-based programs such as MBSR and MBCT (mindfulness-based cognitive therapy) have become increasingly integrated into medicine, health care, and psychology due to the growing evidence base for their efficacy in the lives and health of medical patients with a range of chronic stress-related and pain-related conditions and diseases, as well as people suffering from depression and anxiety. In a parallel emergence, mindfulness and other contemplative practices are now making their way increasingly into the mainstream curriculum in colleges and universities. (9). In primary and secondary schools, as we have seen, bringing mindfulness to both teachers and pupils is in part a response to the increasing stress and challenges faced by children, teachers, and schools that, *in toto*, degrade optimal learning (10).

Introducing mindfulness practices into the classroom at any grade level involves considerable creativity and innovation on the part of the classroom teacher. It is not in the slightest a cookie-cutter, one-size-fits-all approach. Nor is it a covert strategy for behavior management, even though a likely bi-product of it can be a much more effective classroom atmosphere for learning. What Daniel Rechtschaffen offers us here is an effective, user-friendly approach for classroom teachers, one that emphasizes that there is no one right way to teach mindfulness and that it functions best when the teacher is experimenting with using his or her own life as a laboratory for exploring and deepening the practice of mindfulness. The book provides a range of different creative options and approaches for teachers at every grade level who wish to bring this approach into their classrooms with both rigor and playfulness. It is a treasure trove of perspectives and practices that will be useful for years to come to support and inspire classroom teachers and administrators seeking to introduce and integrate mindfulness into various aspects of the curriculum, from kindergarten through high school.

In November 2012, I was walking across a football field that the Middle School shares with the High School at Camp Zama, the sprawling US Army Headquarters in Japan. Out of nowhere, a voice came over the PA system declaring a totally matter-of-fact tone of voice: "The chimes will now signal the beginning of a mindful minute." I could hardly believe my ears. Apparently all the students knew what that meant—they had been training in mindfulness—and dropped into stillness, silence, and awareness for that minute. I learned later that it was the principal of the middle mchool who made the announcement. This came about because a counselor, Jason Kuttner, thought bringing mindfulness into the curriculum would be helpful. Now it is part of the curriculum throughout the middle school, and many of the high school students have been introduced to it as well. This is an example of how one person's intention can make a school-wide difference, just as Cherry Hamrick's did in her school, and so many other teachers, many of whose stories are in the book, are doing as well.

In December of 2013, Chris Ruane, a Member of Parliament in the United Kingdom, and for many years a classroom teacher in Wales, gave a powerful and compelling speech in Parliament addressed directly to the Minister of Education sitting before him in the chamber. The speech, which he entitled *Mindfulness in Education,* aimed to make the case for why the efforts in the UK to bring mindfulness into primary and secondary education is so important, and why all classroom teachers should be offered the opportunity to receive quality training in mindfulness (11). He singled out a number of programs as exemplars, including what is called the ".b" program, a curriculum developed by Mindfulness in Schools, the work of two secondary school teachers, Chris Cullen and Richard Burnett. They have developed imaginative and highly popular approaches for teaching mindfulness in elementary and secondary schools in the UK. Their group has a research program linked to the Oxford University Centre for Mindfulness. It is one of a number of inspiring mindfulness programs that Daniel Rechtschaffen describes. There are many others, both at home and abroad.

If you are a teacher, or an educator, or involved in school administration and curriculum development, the book you hold in your hands has the potential to transform your life, the lives of your students, and the life of the school itself, as well as education in America. I welcome its timely publication. May it be a useful and valuable resource for all teachers who wish to optimize both inner and outer learning and to nurture the unique potential and beauty of each of their students.

Jon Kabat-Zinn
Berkeley, California
January 31, 2014

References

(1) Mindful Schools has since changed their way of working and is now offering training programs in mindfulness to primary and secondary school teachers rather than bringing specialists into the classroom.
(2) see, for example: http://www.mindfulschools.org/about-mindfulness/stories/ - students
(3) see: http://lindastone.net/
(4) Sonia J. Lupien, Bruce S. McEwen, Megan R. Gunnar, and Chris-

tine Heim Effects of stress throughout the lifespan on the brain, behavior and cognition. Nature Reviews Neuroscience (2009) 10: 434-445.

(5) Goleman, D. Emotional Intelligence. Bantam, NY, 1995; see also http://www.cfchildren.org/advocacy/social-emotional-learning/the-cost-of-emotional-illiteracy-part-1.aspx;

(6) see: http://www.cfchildren.org/advocacy/social-emotional-learning/21st-century-skills-vital-for-future-workforce.aspx

(7) Linda Lantieri, personal communication; see also: Lantieri, L. Building Emotional Intelligence: Techniques to Cultivate Inner Strength in Children. Sounds True, Boulder, CO, 2008.

(8) See Mindfulness in the Classroom. In Kabat-Zinn, M. and Kabat-Zinn, J. Everyday Blessings: The Inner Work of Mindful Parenting, Hyperion, New York, 1997; 2014; also, see: http://mindfuleduca tion.org/Mindfulnessintheclassroom-JKZ.pdf

(9) Barbezat, D.P. and Bush, M. Contemplative Practices in Higher Education: Powerful Methods to Transform Teaching and Learning. Jossey-Bass, New York, NY, 2014.

(10) Davidson, R., Dunne, J., Eccles, J. S., Engle, A., Greenberg, M., Jennings, P., Jha, A., Jinpa, T., Lantieri, L., Meyer, D., Roeser, R. W., & Vago, D. (2012). Contemplative Practices and Mental Training: Prospects for American Education. *Child Development Perspectives*. 6(2): 146-153; Roeser, R. W., Schonert-Reichl, K. A., Jha, A., Cullen, M., Wallace, L., Wilensky, R., Oberle, E., Thomson, K., Taylor, C., & Harrison, J. (2013). Mindfulness Training and Reductions in Teacher Stress and Burnout: Results From Two Randomized, Waitlist-Control Field Trials. *Journal of Educational Psychology*. Abstract; Jennifer L. Frank , Patricia A. Jennings & Mark T. Greenberg (2013) Mindfulness-Based Interventions in School Settings: An Introduction to the Special Issue, Research in Human Development, 10:3, 205-210, DOI: 10.1080/15427609.2013 .818480; http://dx.doi.org/10.1080/15427609.2013.818480

(11) see: http://www.theyworkforyou.com/whall/?id=2013-12-10a.66.0

INTRODUCTION

❉

For some reason a particular email from the "White House" looked different than the rest of the political junk mail that so frequently clogs my inbox. It turns out my decision not to send it to the trash was important. "We are pleased to invite you to join Obama administration officials in a roundtable discussion," the message began. They had invited me to represent the mindfulness in education movement, describing the transformational effects these practices are having on our youth.

Before I knew it, I was being screened through the White House gates and sitting with a table of upright army generals, Homeland Security officials, and representatives from the Department of Health and Human Services and a slew of other departments. It has seemed obvious to me from the moment I first tasted the sweet inner stillness of mindfulness 20 years ago that our society could be profoundly transformed if we taught these practices to all children, medical patients, and—why not?—politicians, but I never imagined the government would actually take the leap.

As a family and school therapist, I began teaching the transformative practice of mindfulness to kids in 2006 to help them with anxiety, impulsivity, attention disorders, and depression and to help them cultivate happy and fulfilling lives. I had no idea there was already a mindfulness in education movement under way. Then I learned of organizations such as Mindful Schools teaching in classrooms around the California Bay area, the Mind Body Awareness Project bringing mindfulness to incarcerated youth, and Mindfulness without Borders teaching students around the world. Thrilled that I was not alone, I leapt in and began teaching mindfulness in California classrooms and helping various organizations create mindfulness-based curricula.

Now I have one of those jobs that no one could have imagined 10 years ago. I fly around the world consulting with school systems to help them create mindful, empathic, and inspiring learning environments. One week I'm in Thailand leading an international conference for teachers to bring mindfulness and social emotional learning back to their home countries; the next week I am in Atlanta, consulting with a K–12 school and training their baseball team in attention, embodiment, and team communication; the next week I'm back in California leading a retreat for the educators who are part of the year-long Mindful Education Institute. Luckily I'm teaching mindfulness and know that to teach well I need to perpetually deepen my own presence, openheartedness, and attention, otherwise the pace of my life would really stress me out. At the airport, when I am asked if the trip is business or pleasure I like to give an emphatic, "Yes!"

I teach educators, administrators, and kids the most fundamental principles. If you are teaching someone to drive a car, you need to sit them in the driver's seat and make sure they know the basic rules of the road. In educating children we are training them how to navigate in the world, but we usually skip over the operating manual. How do your minds, hearts, and bodies work? How do we cultivate attention? How do we develop kindness toward ourselves and others? It's rare that schools or parents show children how to cultivate the very ethical attitudes they are espousing, and usually this is because we were never taught these priceless practices ourselves. We may assume that our own happiness is a state that happens to us, rather than a muscle we can exercise into strength and potency. Once we have gained this insight, we can become strength trainers for our students' attention, happiness, and ethical values.

In 2008 I decided to launch the Mindfulness in Education Conference at the Omega Institute, a holistic learning center in Rhinebeck, New York. This annual conference brings together teachers such as Daniel Siegel, Jon Kabat-Zinn, Linda Lantieri, Goldie Hawn, Danny Goleman, Susan Kaiser-Greenland, and many other leaders in the mindfulness and education field. Leading this conference at Omega has a special significance for me, because it was the place I gained my own education in mindfulness.

My parents, Elizabeth Lesser and Stephan Rechtschaffen, founded the Omega Institute in 1977. My mother and father were pioneers in bringing masters of meditation, yoga, and other contemplative traditions to the American public. I have early childhood memories of Shaolin monks standing on sword blades, yogis twisting their bodies into knots, and meditation masters sitting as still as statues for hours. This all seemed normal to me. I was usually backstage with friends, making forts out of meditation cushions, but I must have been listening to the teachings on some level.

I remember toddling into my father's room at four years old and seeing him sitting motionless, cross-legged, on his bed. I stood there for a few moments, confused. There was a stillness I was not accustomed to. I could tell there was something important happening, but he was just sitting, doing nothing.

I stood transfixed until he opened his eyes and gestured for me to come over. I climbed up on the bed for my first mindfulness lesson. He taught me to watch each breath moving in and out. On every in breath I was to count, one, two, three. . . . Every time my mind ran away I was to bring it back and count again from the beginning.

My brother and I tried to turn it into a competition to see who could count the highest without thinking. "I got to 23," I said. "No way, you're lying!" he replied. We realized quickly that there was no way to verify the other's internal experience, and hence no way to turn it into a competitive game. We gave up pretty fast and went back to basketball and checkers, but this first glimpse at the inner working of my mind spurred a lifelong inquiry.

Early on I began asking myself unsettlingly awesome existential questions. Why was I here? What happens when I die? I was one of those kids who had an early hunger to ask the big questions of life and had a mindful environment in which that inquiry could grow. I was gifted with parents and teachers at Omega who would listen to my early cosmic questions with care and insight. However, when I would ask my 10-year-old school friends something like, "What do you think happens to our minds when we die?" I would get scared, frozen faces in response.

Not knowing how to speak to my peers or teachers about what I was experiencing led me to split into two distinct selves.

There was my "social self," who played with friends, watched Saturday morning cartoons, and sat at my little desk memorizing agonizing timetables. I strove to be as normal as an American kid could become. I would watch MTV with a pen and paper, taking notes on how to be cool. I started a rap group in third grade and wore hip-hop gear 10 sizes too large and Air Jordan sneakers. Although my social self found acceptance in the culture of cool, my "authentic self" was longing to be integrated. School was definitely a place that my authentic self felt like a foreigner trying to pass as one of the locals, wondering why no one at school was talking about the big questions.

I have had to cobble together the holistic education my body, mind, and heart were seeking. Studying Western philosophy in college fed my mind but left my heart and body empty and seeking. Graduate school in psychology met my needs for emotional and relational development, but my body remained neglected. Spending time in nature with indigenous teachers, practicing tai chi, and dancing brought me to a deeper sense of embodiment. My mindfulness practice has been the guiding star the entire time, shining awareness on the journey. My life has been a path of integration, my authentic self and my social self gradually becoming one and the same.

In returning to Omega to lead the Mindfulness in Education conference, I realized I was looking to teach the same empathic upbringing I had been raised with. We usually have 300 teachers join us for this weekend of inspiring speakers, practices, and community building. Soon I realized that to really train a teacher to learn an inner mindfulness practice, embody it for their students, and teach skillful lessons, we were going to need a lot longer than a weekend. I ended up leading five-day retreats, which allowed us to dive much deeper, but still, it seemed like attendees needed more. I started the Mindful Education Institute in 2011 as a yearlong teacher training so that participants could have silent mindfulness retreats of a full week and spend a year as a community bringing this into their worlds. This book is an extension of my exploration of how to best serve this growing mindfulness in education movement.

This movement cannot be summed up in a weekend conference, a year of training, or in this book. I am inviting you on a journey to a new paradigm, one where we are learning and teaching with our students, which necessitates admitting that we are all works in progress. Like toddlers learning to walk by toppling over again and again, I offer my own clumsy attempts at being a teacher worth learning from, inviting you to stumble with me into a future so inspiring we cannot yet imagine it. I have taught in hundreds of classrooms around the world, but I have never been a full-time classroom teacher; I am humbled again and gain by how much I don't know. I am striving to be an author without being authoritative. In the same way, I am inviting you to become more of a learning companion than a top-down teacher. With this book I invite you on a collaborative journey with me. You have knowledge and insights beyond my own that we all need to hear. The wisdom of a group is always greater than that of an individual.

I can say with certainty that everything we need to build the compassionate society we all want is already here. It's as if we want a beautiful house and are standing next to a giant pile of wood and tools. I have learned from my time teaching mindfulness practices to kids that even preschoolers can learn impulse control, compassion, attention, communication skills, and stress relief—all of the necessary building materials for a healthy, happy, and responsible life. We have the materials; now we need to build the house.

How This Book Is Organized

Part I is Why Mindful Education Matters. There is a great mindfulness in education movement under way. We begin this journey with an introduction to the work that is already happening and being brought to diverse populations in different formats. We need to go back and ask the obvious question of what mindfulness is. Mindfulness has ancient roots with very modern applications. With cutting-edge research we have taken great strides in understanding the effects that these practices have on the mind, heart, and body. We will look at how mindfulness can support our students and us as teachers.

In Part II, Begin with Yourself, we learn that to teach mindfully, we need to be mindful. There's no way around it. If you are a parent, teacher, therapist, or anyone else with children in your life, the greatest gift you can give to them is your authentic presence. With this in mind, I've devoted the section to teaching you the art of mindfulness so that you can embody the practices with your students. Even if you only read this part of the book, you have the opportunity to transform your classroom. We will also look into some basic psychological foundations of how to become aware of ourselves so that we are not projecting onto our students. From here we will learn to cultivate awareness in our bodies, focus attention, develop compassion, and to be mindful in our everyday lives.

Part III, Cultivating a Mindful Classroom, will discuss how to bring these teachings into the classroom from a place of deepened presence and compassion. We look at the characteristics of a mindful teacher and how to embody our practice with our students. We look at some essential ingredients of creating a mindful classroom, such as council practice, the peace corner, and making classroom agreements.

We examine helpful skills for working with different age groups and how to language these teachings to be most accessible to each developmental stage. We explore cultural diversity and inclusion and how to teach mindfulness in the most appropriate, supportive way. We also examine how stress and trauma affect students and methods to best care for them.

In the final section, Part IV, Mindful Education Curriculum, we finally explore a number of lessons that can be delivered in various settings. We learn how to introduce mindfulness and how to format lessons. These lessons are grouped into four basic types—embodiment, attention, heartfulness, and interconnectedness—and can be adapted for any age group and population. Finally, we learn how to help students integrate mindfulness into their lives. As we bring our mindful attention and compassionate commitment into the world, we help develop the peaceful society we all long for.

This book is an invitation to self-discovery, waking up with a wide-open heart to the world around you, and becoming a skilled purveyor of whole new way of being. I invite you to be courageously hopeful and dedicated with me.

The Way of Mindful Education

PART I

Why Mindful Education Matters

The Way of Mindfulness

❋

Let's begin our exploration of mindfulness with an experiment. Notice your eyes engaging with the letters of this text as you read. At the end of this paragraph, see if you can stop and focus on the letters simply as shapes for a minute, as if you were a baby in awe of the varied forms flowing in through your eyes. Let your eyes and body relax and take in the text as a work of art, letting go of the need to assign meaning to the words.

After you finish reading this paragraph, pause for a moment and try listening to the sounds around you, smelling the smells, sensing the temperature and pulses in your body, without assigning any meaning to your experiences. No labeling the sound as the "heater," or identifying the smell as "pancakes." See if for a few minutes you can simply receive your sensory world like a beautiful symphony.

The process of understanding what mindfulness is begins with firsthand experience. In my initial meeting with any class, I ask the students if anyone has heard of mindfulness. I want to know about their preconceived notions. Years ago the majority of my students had no idea what mindfulness was. Now when I ask, almost everyone raises a hand. The responses range from sage-like definitions to questions like "Isn't that what Oprah does?"

After introducing myself and learning a bit about the students, I invite the class to sit in attentive silence for one minute. Students often finish this period of silence with a sense of amazement, saying something like, "It was so quiet I think I heard the buzz of the light bulbs." They are delighted. They have been in the same classroom for an entire year, and have never heard the noise right above their heads. Within one minute of silence, there it is. In one of my favorite exercises, I lead my students in eating raisins mindfully. Kids say there's as much taste in that tiny bit of food as in eating a whole watermelon. Sometimes students ask, "Is this magic?" It's the kind of magic that instead of tricking the mind by showing it something mysterious and unreal invites you to see how profoundly mysterious reality already is. I frequently say to students, "It's as if we were in the Muggle world of Harry Potter all this time and then all of a sudden, with mindfulness, we realized that there's the whole magical world of Hogwarts all around us."

A wealth of peer-reviewed mindfulness research has been validating what practitioners have known for thousands of years. Practicing mindfulness regularly supports immune function, cognitive development, attention skills, and emotional regulation; promotes happiness; and even makes us more empathic. Mindfulness is being brought into the military, into boardrooms of Fortune 500 companies, and even into the Olympic Games, where you can watch athletes taking calming mindful breaths before their big event. There are other examples of how mindfulness is being used in the culture at large, including Congressman Tim Ryan's weekly congressional mindful sitting group, Chase Bank's "Resource Center for Mindful Spending," and the World Economic Forum at Davos that recently kicked off its annual meeting with the Mindful Leadership Experience. For mindfulness, the time is now.

If mindfulness works so well for adults, imagine how much easier it would be to teach self-love, inner resilience, and non-judgmental awareness right in the beginning of life before the layers of psychological armoring build up. What would our world be like if every child was offered skills for nurturing and developing their hearts, bodies, and minds? The preliminary research on teaching mindfulness to youth is showing us exactly what we would most hope for. Research on mindfulness in youth has been shown to raise test scores, reduce impulsivity, enhance well-being, and build executive functioning.

You may be getting the feeling that mindfulness is the next wonder drug. It has been touted as the cure for everything from attention deficit hyperactivity disorder to chronic pain to depression and from suffering itself. Though scientific results make it look like a magic pill, the difficulty is that we cannot swallow mindfulness with a glass of water; we have to practice diligently to experience its effects. Mindfulness is no anesthetic; we have to feel more instead of less. We may try mindfulness hoping it will make us feel immediately peaceful and happy, but often it forces us even more viscerally into our own anxiousness, fear, and discomfort. Mindfulness invites us to turn our ship of awareness directly into the storm. Its magic is that when we relax our resistance muscles and open up to what is true, here and now, a whole new way of being and teaching unfolds.

When we practice mindfulness, we are not memorizing what someone else has already discovered, we are setting up conditions in which we can observe the direct experiences in our own minds, bodies, and hearts. Defining mindfulness is like try-ing to explain to a child what the word *fun* means. It's easier just to play a game with them and, as they are dancing around gleefully, you can say, "This is called having fun." Instead of telling you what mindfulness is, I'll ask you a few questions.

- Have you ever been playing sports, making music, or cre-ating art, when all your thoughts seemed to move into the background and you were totally absorbed in the present activity?
- Have you ever been in a dangerous situation where your senses became highly attuned and your attention was laser focused?
- Have you ever looked into the eyes of a baby and felt yourself dumbstruck with love and wonder?
- Have you ever become engrossed in a story where some complete stranger's successes felt like your successes, their hardships were your hardships, their joy was your joy?

In these kinds of moments, our awareness is rooted in the present moment without our minds getting involved with judg-ments and comparisons. These moments of awareness often arise spontaneously, but we practice mindfulness so that we can cultivate it not just in extreme cases but in our normal everyday moments. If you are walking, and are aware of the touch of your feet on the ground and the audiovisual stimuli streaming in as you walk, then you are mindfully walking. If you are driving a car and are aware of the road signs zooming by and the feel of the wheel in your hands, then you are mindfully driving. As simple as this sounds, just think of how many times you may have arrived at a destination across town and realized that you were consumed in thoughts the entire ride. Being mindful could save your life.

Mindfulness is not some new-fangled invention. You don't need to construct this awareness for your students or yourself; we are born with it. In fact, in some ways, children are far more mindful than adults. A child gazing with wide-eyed wonder at ants on a leaf is a clear example of mindful attention. As babies emerge into the world, everything is brand new and miraculous. Of course, everything is still miraculous 20, 30, or 40 years later, but our adult minds somehow learn to make the mysterious mundane. Developmental neuropsychology shows that the brain of an infant is twice as active and adaptive as it is when a person reaches the age of 18. Just as the child playing peek a boo believes that the world disappears behind his hands, adults seem to trick themselves into thinking that just because they have restricted their breadth of awareness, the wide-open world is gone. Somehow we can fly over snow-capped mountains in an airplane, bored, only glancing up occasionally from our sudoku puzzle. It's all too easy to spend our time planning, worrying, and fiddling around on our gadgets while the magnificence of life passes by.

It's never too late to experience the mystery and exhilaration of life. Mindfulness invites us back to the preciousness of the present moment. Kids are already immersed in the present moment, and I am mostly interested in not squashing the bright awareness that is already there. I begin by telling students that we are going to "play mindfulness." There's no homework, no tests, and no way you could possibly get it wrong. By the time we have become adults, most of us have been thoroughly schooled to think that to be loved we need get all the answers right. The mindful way is to unravel some of these old standards so that we can feel happy exactly as we are. For adults mindfulness returns us to direct engagement with the present moment, like you were kneeling down on one knee and getting engaged to this moment, and saying yes!

The Mindful
Education Revolution

Sitting on his bunk bed, locked behind juvenile detention bars, 17-year-old Damon feels his breath softly rising and falling. As another angry thought surfaces, he remembers his mindfulness lesson and notices the tension in his body. He smiles at the passing thought and feels his whole body relax. He notices an inner spaciousness and a sense of freedom that he's not sure he's felt before.

Across town eight-year-old Susan walks to the peace corner in her classroom. She is aware of anxious sensations in her heart and throat—the same feelings she has every time she takes a test. She sits on a comfy cushion, closes her eyes, and imagines she is getting a big hug. The tightness loosens, and a warmth spreads through her body.

As Susan's teacher, Nia, walks into a meeting with the school's vice principal, she uses mindful breathing to stay centered and calm amid the swirling thoughts and feelings as she remembers their past disagreements about discipline and punishment. This time, to her surprise, the vice principal is asking for advice. How is it that Nia's class has gotten the best test scores and yet is the only one that doesn't seem stressed? "Is it this mindfulness thing? Can you teach the rest of us how to do it?"

As you read these words, students from Rwanda to Israel to Jamaica and throughout the United States and Canada are exercising their attention muscles, they are opening their hearts to gratitude and forgiveness, they are learning to relax and to love themselves. Meanwhile teachers are getting the inner resources they desperately need, learning self-compassion, stress-relief, and invaluable lessons to teach their students. They are gaining the inner calm and compassionate attention that can make teaching the passionate profession that originally inspired them. This movement begins within each of our hearts and can transform the entire world.

Doesn't every one of us—teachers, parents, and children—want to feel relaxed rather than stressed, happy rather than depressed, attentive rather than distracted? Don't we want to feel balanced in our mind, hearts, and bodies? Of course we do. It feels better that way.

Students are told to pay attention a thousand times in school, but rarely are they taught how. We tell our kids to be nice to each other again and again, without ever teaching them the incredibly accessible exercises that cultivate empathy and forgiveness. We tell students not to be so reactive and even put them in juvenile detention centers all because they can't regulate the disturbances within their own bodies. There are methods for teaching impulse control, attention, and empathy, but young people have rarely been taught them. Mindfulness has been effectively training these qualities for millennia, and there is a mounting research base that backs up its immense health benefits.

Many in the education field are now looking to mindfulness

as an antidote to the escalating dysregulation of the youth in our society. The statistics are disturbing, and they validate the concerns of teachers and parents alike. The rates of severe psychological disorders have spiked at younger and younger ages. The National Institute of Mental Health reports, "Approximately one in every four to five youth in the U.S. meets criteria for a mental disorder with severe impairment across their lifetime" (Merikangas et al., 2010). We can look at health factors in nearly every arena and see the same accelerating imbalance. Obesity, autism, attention deficit disorder, anxiety, depression, bullying—whether it is social, psychological, or physical, the trends are moving in an unsettling direction.

We can listen to experts in the fields of education, developmental psychology, and neuroscience, but the most important people we need to listen to are our children. Our kids are the canaries in the coalmine, the most vulnerable members of our society, responding to the stressors of our world. What is unaddressed in adult society rears its head in the sandbox games our children play. When I work with young children in my therapy practice, I invite them to play with a vast assortment of little figurines in a sand tray. Invariably the worlds and scenarios the children create represent the unresolved emotional experiences of their lives. A child of domestic violence puts a baby in a crib surrounded by wolves; a child whose parents are getting divorced chooses two houses and places a wall between them. The children represent their inner emotional state in symbols and then play with them to try to find resolution. The stressors children are raised with form the architecture of their very brains and bodies, influencing who they will be for the rest of their lives.

As children overhear the daily news of school shootings,

wars, and ocean levels rising, their minds and bodies are developing amid this myriad of stressors. When the stress levels are high, children sound an alarm with their dysregulation. I hear this alarm in the serious depression and anxiety in my young psychotherapy clients. I heard this alarm loud and clear from a roaring applause in a recent mindfulness assembly I was leading for 150 high school seniors. What about mindfulness, you may ask, would elicit a standing ovation from teenagers?

After a 10-minute silent breathing practice, a young woman in the assembly audience asked an important question. "As I was sitting I was almost falling asleep. What do I do about that?" "Are you tired?" I asked. "Whenever I stop doing stuff, I crash," she said. When I asked what she was so busy doing, she gave me an exasperated laundry list of classwork, extracurricular activities, and family and social engagements. I responded, "We all have so much we are doing for school, for our parents, to look cool with our friends, that deep down we are bone tired. It's not that mindfulness makes us tired, it's that mindfulness shows us how tired we actually are." The whole room seemed to be nodding in unison. "Perhaps we should reinstitute nap time from preschool into every grade, " I suggested.

Big smiles appeared on the students' faces and then clapping, hooting, and eventually the standing ovation. A standing ovation for nap time? These students, and other students around the world, are profoundly stressed. Whether it is in the impoverished Oakland schools where I work or in progressive prep schools, students are crying out for calm. They need an environment in which their nervous systems can relax and feel nourished. In my psychotherapy practice and in my travels to schools around the world I always ask kids if they enjoy being in school. Sadly the majority of them look at me quizzically, as if the possibility of enjoying school never occurred to them.

As an adult I still sometimes awaken from terrified dreams about being back in school, unprepared for a test. When our nervous systems are on high alert, or when we are flushed with self-critical thoughts, then our working memories function poorly, our creative juices do not flow, and our collaborative capacities are stymied. The premise of mindful education is that all human beings are born with the seeds of the most beneficial universal qualities, such as compassion, creativity, integrity, and wisdom. From this perspective the ideal of education is to teach in such a way that fosters these beautiful latent qualities. Instead of creating an atmosphere of stress, competition, and punishment, we create an atmosphere of acceptance, care, and encouragement. We start by honoring children exactly as they are; when they receive this type of attention, children can grow to their fullest human potential. As any teacher knows, when a student feels safe, relaxed, and attentive, learning comes naturally.

When the teenagers were applauding for nap time, I thought of the movement in high school education to push the start of the school day a bit later. It turns out that biologically it is healthier for teens to wake up later. It's not that they are lazy and obstinate; rather, they are answering an inner biological call. With this in mind, two schools in Minnesota agreed to push the school day back, and there was a significant reduction in school dropout rates, less depression, and higher grades (Wahlstrom, 2002). Any teenager in the world could tell you that they naturally need to go to sleep later and wake up later. All we had to do was ask.

When we don't listen to our students, we are in a perpetual battle against them. When we don't honor the amount of physical movement kids need, we have to fight them or medicate them into sitting at a desk all day. When we don't offer students a healthy way to express difficult emotions, we end up being perpetually frustrated by their behaviors. When we don't teach them how to pay attention, we end up yelling at them when they are distracted. So many teachers have expressed grief to me because they feel as if they are in a war with the very kids they want to help.

Year after year I have watched schoolteachers entering the classroom on the first day as hopeful and inspired as a child taking its first steps. But sadly, by the end of the year, the teacher is often beleaguered, crawling toward the final day. The National Commission on Teaching and America's Future reports that 46 percent of all new teachers in the United States leave the profession within five years. They report, "In 1987–88 the typical teacher had 15 years of experience, but by 2007–08 the typical teacher had just 1 to 2 years of experience" (Black, Neel, & Benson, 2008). The teacher drop-out rate is worse than the drop-out rate for children. Before any good teaching and learning can happen, we need to cultivate environments where children and teachers aren't running for the exits. We need to nourish the inner lives of our students *and* teachers.

The History of
Mindful Education

❋

After World War II the World Health Organization commissioned psychologist John Bowlby to study the psychological health of Europe's children. Part of his professional recommendations read, "The infant and young child should experience a warm, intimate, and continuous relationship with his mother (or permanent mother substitute) in which both find satisfaction and enjoyment" (Bowlby, 1951). You may find nothing revelatory about this quote; what is shocking about this statement is how revolutionary an idea it was to parents and teachers at the time. There was a great fight against Bowlby's idea that children needed warmth and affection to grow into healthy adults. Many assumed that as long as food and shelter were provided, the child would be fine. If the child had emotional or behavioral problems, it was not connected to the possible neglect or abuse they had received. As research progresses we see more and more how a child's emotional environment is key in the development of not only physical and emotional health but also academic and worldly success.

It's not that the idea of having an empathic presence when teaching children had never been thought of before. Educational visionaries like Maria Montessori and Rudolph Steiner recommended experiential and emotionally responsive teaching before Bowlby ever published his study. If we look all the way back at the roots of language, we see that the word *learn* comes from the same etymological root of *footprint* and *track*. At one time all of our ancestors learned not in square desks but following animal tracks through open prairies and forests. We learned not *about* the stars, animals, and elements but *from* them. Imagine yourself as a child following your parents through the streams and thickets, learning the prints of deer, fox, and bear. Take your child to work day was every day. Originally education was purely sensory, relational, and a wholly mindful experience.

Although some teachers have always understood the necessity for a holistic education, the main current of public schooling has done very little to address the full spectrum of emotional, social, physical, and other aspects of the "whole child." In the early 1980s Howard Gardener posited his "multiple intelligences theory" (Gardner, 1983). This theory sees humans as having nine relatively independent arenas of intelligence, each of which needs to be exercised and nourished. The nine types are linguistic, logic-mathematical, musical, spatial, bodily, interpersonal, intrapersonal, naturalistic, and existential. In remembering the importance of all these neglected human aspects, we are also becoming aware of the aspects within ourselves that may have been neglected in our own schooling and homes.

As more of an interpersonal, intrapersonal, naturalistic, and existential thinker, I always felt like I wasn't smart enough in school. Because of the logic-mathematical-minded school system I was raised in, I would think, "maybe there's something wrong with me." How many children like me, who are not memorization or mathematically minded, feel disempowered, miss the boat, and then feel as though they are trailing behind for years. It was deeply liberating when I was privileged enough later in life to study philosophy, psychology, and meditation and learn, to my great astonishment that I naturally excelled in this type of learning.

Emotional intelligence, a term popularized by Daniel Goleman, has shifted the educational dialogue from strictly looking at IQ to EQ (emotional quotient). Goleman's work helped support the Social Emotional Learning (SEL) movement, which had been bringing values-based educational learning into schools since the late 1960s, beginning at the Yale School of Medicine's Child Study Center. SEL programs have become prevalent around the world, and in many of the largest U.S. school districts and have been shown to support emotional regulation, social competency, and resiliency as well as increase academic achievement by 11 percent (Durlak, Weissberg, Dymnicki, Taylor, & Schellinger, 2011).

SEL programs support students in developing these five social emotional competencies:

- Self-management
- Self-awareness
- Social awareness
- Relationship skills
- Responsible decision making

One of the leading visionaries of the SEL movement is Linda Lantieri, the director of the Inner Resilience Program and founding board member of the Collaborative for Academic, Social, and Emotional Learning (CASEL). I led a discussion with Lantieri, Goleman, and neuroscience author and psychiatry professor Daniel Siegel at the Mindfulness in Education conference at the Omega Institute. Lantieri and Goleman talked at length about their initial conversations 20 years ago forming what is now CASEL. I was inspired to ask these two visionaries, who helped transform the heart of education through SEL, what role mindfulness could play in the future of education.

The answer was clear. They discussed the core competencies of SEL and went on to explain how mindfulness practices are the best ways to cultivate these competencies. Siegel gave a synthesis of everything we had been saying about SEL and mindfulness in one word: *integration.*

He brought together all of the profound information Goleman and Lantieri had shared about mindfulness and its effects on attention, emotion, and behavior and explained it through the lens of neuroscience. He described how mindfulness practices support the integration of separated functional areas of the brain, linking them with synaptic connections. When mindfulness links the brain up in this way, the five competencies of self-management, self-awareness, social awareness, relationship skills, and responsible decision making naturally arise.

Instead of telling children to be kind, attentive, and balanced, practicing mindfulness actively fosters these qualities. With this in mind, many SEL programs are integrating mindfulness as the training ground for their ethics and values-based curriculum. Mindfulness can support and be woven into the great wisdom of social emotional learning, multiple intelligence theory, and many other conscious education philosophies. Instead of pushing aside educational paradigms that have come before, mindfulness supports the cognitive, emotional, physical, and relational aspects of learning.

Mapping the Movement

※

For many years in the mindfulness in education community, we have asked ourselves the question of how best to deliver mindfulness-based curricula. We've arrived at three main approaches to introducing mindfulness in youth-based settings. Many schools, organizations, after-school programs, juvenile detention centers, therapy centers, and other institutions are learning to integrate these invaluable practices. In learning to create a mindful classroom environment for our students, we will find it useful to take a look at the approaches others have taken. The three main forms have been:

- Training and self-care for teachers
- Direct service to students
- Curriculum-based teaching

Training and Self-Care for Teachers

Many organizations focus exclusively on the cultivation of mindfulness in the teachers. The trainings help teachers with self-care. The vision is that the teacher's sense of well-being will naturally translate into an environment of wellness for the students. The trainings that are based on working primarily with teachers work from the belief that mindfulness is only truly taught through the transmission of an experienced practitioner. People in this camp often look with frustration at the mindfulness-based curricula for sale, because teachers who use them may teach the exercises without ever having done mindfulness practices themselves. Imagine a teacher banging a bell and yelling at kids to be still and relaxed. Instead of teaching kids to liberate their minds, this could become mindfulness in the name of control and obedience.

The format for these trainings can be as simple as a professional development time where teachers get massages and are taught relaxation techniques. Other programs are full year-long trainings where participants experience silent, five-day mindfulness retreats and are given progressive instruction in embodiment, mind training, and emotional intelligence.

Caring for yourself is always a good idea. Resources and time are often an obstacle for schools, and longer trainings can be expensive and hard for educators to afford. Finding a way to offer these teachings to all caregivers in an economically accessible form is an important concern for this movement.

Some organizations that take this approach: Inner Resilience Program, CARE for Teachers, SMART in Education, and Parker Palmer's Courage and Renewal Programs.

Direct Service to Students

Many organizations offer direct services provided by experienced mindfulness practitioners. These outside trainers go into juvenile detention halls, schools, and after-school programs to teach mindfulness practices directly. There has also been an inspiring new trend of schools hiring for an internal position of social emotional learning/mindfulness director. This teacher visits classrooms to lead trainings and often has an office that groups and individuals can visit for extra mindfulness time.

Organizations that deliver direct service programs intentionally hire teachers with a depth of experience and teaching skill, who can often transmit the practices in a very inspiring way. Cultivating a deep mindfulness practice can take great diligence, and learning how to communicate these practices is a real art, so there is great benefit to using experienced mindfulness teachers.

The problem with direct service is that often these amazing teachers open up new ways of seeing the world for kids, but then they leave. There can be a lack of systemic change with direct service, and there can even be a danger of kids developing an authenticity that instead of being reinforced can be judged or suppressed by a community that has not yet built an adequate container. If the classroom teacher is not supportive of mindfulness, then the outside provider's lessons may be directly contrary to the way the teacher directs the class.

Some examples of organizations that take this approach: Mind Body Awareness Project, Holistic Life Foundation, Mindful Schools, the Lineage Project.

Curriculum-Based Teaching

The third view is that mindfulness lessons are inherently supportive for the emotional, mental, and physical development of all children. In this approach the lessons that teach children to breathe, become aware of their thought patterns, and relax into their bodies are inherently helpful even if coming from a teacher without thorough training. The view is that the lessons should be laid out in as conscious a way as possible. This viewpoint has resulted in a proliferation of mindfulness-based curricula for students of all ages and demographics, some of which can be bought online and used without any previous training.

Mindfulness practices have also begun to be incorporated into larger SEL curricula as well as large school systems internationally. There are many basic mindfulness concepts and practices that are being woven into antibullying campaigns, test preparation, and other student-based learning projects.

Some examples of organizations that take this approach: Mind Up Curriculum, .b curriculum, Learning to BREATHE Curriculum, Stress Reduction Workbook for Teens.

All of the Above

As always, it's never that one side is right and the other is wrong. We need a multifaceted approach to integrating these practices into work with youth. Of course we need to begin with caring for and training the teachers. Of course it is helpful to bring in experienced mindfulness teachers to guide the way and mentor the movement. Of course curriculum is incredibly useful to support educators in learning how to integrate these practices into their settings. Even those who would never have thought to practice mindfulness are now getting a taste of it, so let's make sure we are offering them a piece of cake rather then throwing it in their face.

An example of an integrated approach to mindfulness in education is the South Burlington School District in Vermont. I have led several multiple-day mindfulness retreats for their teachers and administrators. They have also brought Linda Lantieri and various other mindfulness and SEL experts for professional development trainings. Their teachers and school therapists have integrated mindfulness curricula into K–12 schools so that children receive these lessons every year as they pass from elementary up through high school graduation. I have also taught in their elementary, middle, and high school classrooms and had their teachers shadow me so they could learn the lessons directly. They have committed to the well-being of their teachers and then give curriculum resources for the teachers to deliver. This is integration in action.

The Science of Mindfulness

❋

The great neuroscientists of ancient history, having no scanning technology, sat still and witnessed the passing phenomenon of their minds, hearts, and bodies. One classic mindfulness technique, the body scan, could be seen as an internal scanner. During a body scan we pass awareness from head to toe, scanning the same phenomena that the neuroscientists are reading on their screens. When I began doing the mindful body scan practice, I very quickly experienced a deep relaxation, focused attention, and an emotional balancing. I didn't need a scientist to tell me what was happening, I was watching the transformation with an inner lens.

Mindfulness is an inner science, and we use our own minds, hearts, and bodies for the research. Instead of a cold scientific study, we examine our inner lives with compassion and tenderness. This inquiry into what makes us tick can offer personal insights as well as a greater sense of self-love.

The other form of scientific research, conducted in labs and academic institutions, is objectively coming to the same conclusions about mindfulness that practitioners have known for thousand of years. Neuroscientists, medical doctors, and even geneticists are showing that mindfulness cultivates attention, compassion, happiness, and relaxation and decreases impulsivity, anxiety, and other difficult emotional states.

I offer here a brief synopsis of some of the science that is pertinent to our exploration of mindfulness in education. I start by looking at the wealth of mindfulness research that has been conducted for the benefit of adults, especially for teachers. It's my hope that this research inspires you to cultivate your own mindfulness practice and gives you invaluable knowledge to share with your colleagues.

Proven Benefits

The number of scientific literature articles published on mindfulness per year has spiked in the last 30 years from 1 in 1982 to 477 in 2012 (Mindful Research Guide, 2013).

When Jon Kabat-Zinn started the Stress Reduction Clinic at the Massachusetts Medical Center in 1979, the word *mindfulness* was nowhere in the medical lexicon. At the clinic Kabat-Zinn developed a program called Mindfulness-Based Stress Reduction (MBSR), which at first was seen as a fringe healing modality. How could breathing and loving yourself help medical patients?

Kabat-Zinn convinced the doctors to send their "treatment-resistant" patients to the Stress Reduction Clinic. In other words, the clinic got all of the patients that Western medicine had no idea how to treat. After practicing mindfulness for eight weeks, these "treatment-resistant" patients started having remarkable transformations. The MBSR patients began finding dramatic symptom reduction in conditions such as high blood pressure, psoriasis, and fibromyalgia. People with chronic pain disorders experienced meaningful reductions in their pain and suffering, and across the board patients reported a greater sense of well-being (Kabat-Zinn, 1982, 1985, 1987).

Doctors now estimate that 60 to 80 percent of the clients they see are coming in with stress-related concerns (Rosch, 1997). Migraines, insomnia, high blood pressure, heart attacks, heart disease, anxiety disorders, depression, and a vast array of our most common ailments are stress-related. Yet only 3 percent of primary care office visits incorporate stress management counseling (Nerurkar, Yeh, Davis, Birdee, & Phillips, 2011).

As profound as Western medicine proves to be every time we take antibiotics for infections that would otherwise kill us, it often doesn't help with more systemic health concerns. Similar to our education system, our medical establishment has rarely looked at the whole patient. But similar to our education system, there is a great shift under way. Medical science is realizing that the health of the patient depends on integrating mind, heart, and body.

The following examples show just a few of the remarkable health benefits that mindfulness research has been proving.

- Body: Mindfulness has been shown to address physical health problems directly and is effective in reducing pain and high blood pressure and improving the symptoms of physical conditions such as psoriasis and fibromyalgia. Mindfulness practice has even been correlated to slowing the rate of cellular aging. Telomorase activity, a predictor of long-term cellular viability, was found to be significantly greater in long-term mindfulness practitioners. (Jacobs et al., 2011).

- Mind: Neuroscience research is showing that mindfulness can positively transform the architecture and operation of the brain, improving sustained attention, visuospatial memory, working memory, and concentration (Jha, Krompinger, & Baime, 2007; Chambers, Chuen Yee Lo, Allen, 2008; Zeidan, Johnson, Diamond, David, & Goolkasian, 2010). Practicing mindfulness can increase blood flow to and create a thickening of the cerebral cortex in areas associated with attention and emotional integration (Davidson et al., 2003). Research on mindfulness practitioners has shown a reduction in gray matter density in the amygdala correlated with a decrease in stress and anxiety (Hölzel et al., 2011).
- Heart: Mindfulness research has been shown to promote the ability to feel in control, make meaningful relationships, accept experience without denying the facts, manage difficult feelings, and be calm, resilient, compassionate, and empathic (Salmon et al., 2004). Mindfulness as a psychological intervention is proving effective in addressing substance abuse, stress, anxiety, and recurrent depression and improving sleep (Baer, 2003). Mindfulness-Based Cognitive Therapy (MBCT) has proven more effective than antidepressants in reducing depressive symptoms and improving well-being (Kuyken et al., 2008).
- Interconnectedness: In one study, participants were unknowingly presented with a staged scene in a waiting room to measure their compassion responses. When an actor on crutches hobbled in, a control group responded compassionately 15 percent of the time, while mindfulness-trained participants responded compassionately 50 percent of the time. It seems that mindfulness can even

make people nicer (Condon et al., 2013)! Last but not least, mindfulness has been shown to enhance auditory focus and make music more enjoyable to listen to (Diaz, 2013). Not only can mindfulness make us kinder people, it helps us enjoy our lives.

Benefits for Teachers, Parents, and Youth Care Providers

Teachers, parents, and other youth care providers have an unusually high degree of stress and burnout. "Compassion fatigue" is a concept that refers to the way we can overextend our caregiving without getting the adequate support we need. The problem is that when we are perpetually trying to help others but not taking care of ourselves, we get exhausted, we burn out, and we are not able to do our jobs at full capacity.

Many trainings are now being offered that focus on supporting teachers' mindfulness practice and self-care. The Stress Management and Resilience Training (SMART), Cultivating Awareness and Resilience in Education (CARE), and a growing body of other mindfulness-based teacher trainings are now being studied with very promising results. For example, schoolteachers who underwent an eight-week mindfulness training at the University of California San Francisco experienced a decrease in anxiety, stress, and depression, while experiencing an increase in compassion and other positive states of mind. Five months after the end of training, these benefits remained for those who had stayed engaged with the practices. Margaret Kemeny, the lead author of the study, says, "We were able to see that the intervention had changed emotions and behaviors in provocative situations, which is most exciting, it is fine if someone is acting happily and compassionately in a positive situation, but if a person is provoked, then acts compassionately and with less anger, it means so much more" (Kemeny et al., 2012). The research seemed to find that teachers who had gone through the training had a greater capacity to experience the inevitable stressors of teaching and maintain an emotional balance, responding not from their reactivity but from an empathic focus.

Benefits of a Mindful Environment

In the most current neuroscience, genetics, attachment psychology, and developmental theory, there is clear agreement that the best thing for a developing child is love, attention, and constancy. The amount and quality of empathic attention children receive wires their brains in either healthy or destructive ways. A well-functioning holding environment supports the child's inner executive functioning.

As Alison Gopnik says in *The Scientist in the Crib*, "Everything a baby hears sees, tastes, touches, and smells influences the way the brain gets hooked up" (Gopnik, Meltzoff, & Kuhl, 2000). Our childhood environment sets up the ways our neural pathways fire together, creating the paths that we walk down in our lives. Research clearly shows that highly stressful environments of neglect and abuse create deficits in children's working memory, attention, and inhibitory control skills (Maughan & Cicchetti, 2002; O'Connor, Rutter, Beckett, Keaveney, & Kreppner, 2000). As babies we are wired relationally. Through gestures, facial expressions, babbling, and other interactions, babies look to the world to build their interpersonal brains. Babies build their own brain architecture through an interplay with their caregivers. When parents or institutions neglect the basic interpersonal needs of the baby, serious detriments can occur to the brain and even the physical system. As the National Scientific Council on the Developing Child says, "Severe neglect in both family and institutional settings are associated with greater risk for emotional, behavioral, and interpersonal relationship difficulties later in life" (National Scientific Council on the Developing Child, 2012).

If a child's early life is marked with comfort, dependability, and nourishment, he or she gains an inner sense of trust and can look to the world with optimism. If the conditions are not safe and nurturing, the child is imprinted with a sense of mistrust and the world becomes a dangerous and undependable place. Primarily because of our level of support and nurturing, we are lead down very different roads. We all know which road we want to be on, which road we want our children to be on, and which way we want our whole world to be headed.

The hope is that when we learn to embody our own mindful attention, compassion, and emotional regulation, the children in our care will receive the relational nourishment they need to become healthy and happy adults. We've all had the experience of a child falling down and looking up to us, basically asking us what the appropriate response should be. We look with a scared face and the child starts wailing, or, we look with calm and focused attention and the child realizes they are fine and goes back to playing.

To take this a step further, Joe Campos of the of the University of California Berkeley Infant Studies Center, created an experiment in which children could see their mothers and crawled toward them until they reached a visual cliff (Campos, Langer, & Krowitz, 1970).

There was actually glass over the expanse that the child could climb over, but it looked like a perilous fall. Some mothers were told to look with total confidence and smiles, whereas others were told to keep blank, cold faces. The children who looked at the blank-faced moms stayed frozen at the edge, while the ones who looked in the encouraging eyes of their mothers walked right over the glass—walking on air.

Imagine how nice it would have been if your parents and teachers had never put any of their own irrational fears or unmet needs onto you when you were a child. Imagine that your friends and family could see you exactly as you are without wanting you to be a certain way or projecting their fears and wishes on you. Imagine for a second how your whole body would respond to a world of encouragement and trust. Now imagine what such a world would be like for your students and children.

How Mindfulness Benefits Our Students

Current neuroscience and developmental psychology can help us understand the benefits and usefulness of mindfulness training in the lives of children. Let's start by looking at a common three-part division of our brains: the instinctual reptilian brain, the emotional mammalian brain, and the creative and logical neocortex. As our brains have evolved, they have built on the scaffolding of prior evolutionary development. In a very literal way, we still have a part of us that has the survival focus of a lizard, a part that has the highly social attention of a dog, and this relatively new part of the brain that sips espresso while reading the *New York Times*. Even young children can understand this concept, and as part of their mindfulness training they can learn how their neuroscience effects their behaviors and choices.

The old reptilian and mammalian parts of the brain motivate us through pleasure and fear and have supported our survival for millennia. Through our evolution we have reached a point where our neocortex wraps around our brain, making up 80 percent of its mass. Though the neocortex may be the bulk of the brain, the old brain is still a serious force. Your rational brain may know that eating that ice cream cone is not healthy, but how often does the lizard take control and eat it anyway? Our brains are kind of like a family road trip. Often when we are angry or upset, the baby part of us ends up behind the wheel and our adult part is freaking out in the backseat. It's not that we need to get rid of the baby; we need to learn to put the adult in the driver's seat and the baby safely in the carseat. We cannot get rid of any of these parts, nor would we want to, because they are all essential to integrating a full, healthy human being.

Daniel Siegel, author of *The Mindful Brain*, has written extensively on how mindfulness helps children in integrating their brains. In *The Whole-Brain Child* he writes:

> We want to help our children become better integrated so they can use their whole brain in an integrated way. For example, we want them to be horizontally integrated, so that their left brain logic can work with their right brain emotion. We also want them to be vertically integrated, so that the physically higher parts of their brain, which let them thoughtfully consider their actions, work well with lower

parts, which are more concerned with instinct, gut reactions, and survival (Siegel & Bryson, 2011).

In practicing mindfulness, we can learn to effectively integrate these different parts of the brain and mediate the internal conflicts. There is a basic neuroscience concept: "Nerve cells that fire together, wire together." Due to recent findings of neural plasticity, which is the ability for the connections in our brains to change and adapt throughout our lives, we now understand that our brains can generate stronger and healthier neural connections based on our mental habits. Mindfulness trains our brains to respond in ways we choose instead of always in a default manner, which often is a knee-jerk reptilian reaction. This is especially pertinent in situations that bring up stress or conflict. For instance, if a child has learned to use violence to react to feeling scared, mindfulness can help him or her become aware of this habitual behavior and the feelings underneath it, and ultimately rewire the reaction to a constructive and positive one.

Studies have shown that long-term mindfulness practitioners actually grow thicker prefrontal cortexes, this being the brain region responsible for executive functioning (EF). Developmental neuroscientists studying the effects of mindfulness on executive functioning say, "Mindfulness-based interventions that focus on increasing awareness of one's thoughts, emotions, and actions have been shown to improve specific aspects of EF, including attention, cognitive control, and emotion regulation" (Tang, Yang, Leve, & Harold, 2012). This means that through mindfulness, students can learn to pay better attention in class, regulate their emotions, and develop stronger social fluency. Through mindful breathing, walking, and compassion practices, kids can develop the neural linkages that foster a healthy life.

Although the field of mindfulness in education is still young, there has been a flurry of research on the effects of mindfulness in classrooms, juvenile detention centers, and other youth-based centers. Most of the research is still in preliminary phases, but the results are pointing to the promising goals we all hope for. Positive attributes such as the ability to emotionally self-regulate, demonstrate empathy, pay attention, and exhibit improved executive functioning go up, while destructive tendencies such as impulsivity, violence, and stress go down. Many studies still need to be done to see which practices are effective at which ages and to which effects, but here is a sample of what we have already learned.

- A 24-week mindfulness training with a group of first-, second-, and third-graders resulted in improvement on attention tasks and significant improvements in symptoms of ADHD (Napoli, Krech, & Holley, 2005).
- A mindfulness training was conducted for students in Belgium aimed at reducing depression. The findings suggest that school-based mindfulness programs can help reduce and prevent depression in adolescents (Raes, Griffith, Van der Gucht, & Williams, 2013).
- A mindfulness-based stress reduction program, adapted for teens, found that those receiving MBSR self-reported reduced symptoms of anxiety, depression, and somatic distress and increased self-esteem and sleep quality (Biegel, Warren Brown, Shapiro, & Schubert, 2009).
- In juvenile detention centers, one study showed significantly reduced hostility and emotional discomfort in its

incarcerated population after mindfulness training. These incarcerated youth improved in interpersonal relationships, school achievement, and stress after going through the training (Sibinga et al., 2011).

- In a groundbreaking study, it was found that "mindfulness training improved both GRE reading-comprehension scores (by an average of 16%) and working memory capacity, while simultaneously reducing the occurrence of distracting thoughts during completion of the GRE and the measure of working memory" (Mrazek, Franklin, Tarchin Phillips, Baird, & Schooler, 2013).

Research like this is beginning to show us the extent to which mindfulness offers students the key ingredients to living a healthy, happy, and successful life. From a results-based perspective, we are pleased to see that mindfulness raises test scores and reduces behavioral problems. What is most inspiring to me is the way I see children, through mindfulness, learning to feel fully comfortable in their own skins, trust themselves, and be compassionate to the world around them. Even more than raising test scores, I hope for an entire generation of students cultivating compassion for themselves and others. If a child's mind is wired by his or her relationships with caregivers, then imagine our children becoming even more integrated than we are, and their children becoming even more integrated, and moving in the direction of a peaceful, integrated society.

The Origins of Mindfulness

✳

Mindfulness does not belong to Christianity, Buddhism, or Taoism, just as the breath we inhale and exhale does not belong to any one of us. Everywhere human beings have lived, we have needed to cultivate attention; whether it was for hunting, fashioning tools or clothes, or intellectual pursuits. We have always needed compassion to live in harmony and enjoy our lives. Humans from every culture have developed wisdom to ask the big questions of life. These universal practices have been cultivated throughout millennia—or, we may say, they have cultivated us.

Throughout history religious and cultural traditions around the world have used meditation to build on the capacities of authenticity, kindness, and insight. Many religious traditions use the deities of their particular religion, using visualizations, mantras, and prayer to cultivate these characteristics. For our purposes we will not use any practices with language from religious cosmologies, although there can be great merits to those practices. The beauty of mindfulness for our modern use is that all we need is our breath, our bodies, our minds, and our hearts.

Every cultural and religious tradition has its own mindfulness practices. If you come from a tradition to which you feel connected, I recommend exploring the practices within it. The prayers, meditations, and devotional practices you can find in any tradition can be used to cultivate compassion, attention, and a sense of connection to all things. The mindfulness practices set out in this book can also focus and support the practices of whichever tradition you are already part of. Steady focus and an open heart can support the prayers of a Christian, the poses of a yogi, and the intellectual questioning of an atheist.

I have had several experiences in which parents or teachers expressed concern that my colleagues and I were teaching Buddhism in the schools. Each time this has happened, I have invited the parent or teacher to see for themselves and sit in on one of the classes. Once they have seen that all we are doing is learning to breathe, relax, and find emotional equilibrium, no one has complained any further. In fact, a few of these parents and administrators have become major supporters of the mindfulness in education movement. Mindfulness-based curricula and trainings have been fluidly instituted into Catholic schools, Jewish schools, Quaker schools, and many other public and private school-based settings.

Nevertheless, separation of church and state is a concern that arises in school settings, and it is important to address. Buddhism as a tradition has spent a great deal of time on the universal practices of attention and loving kindness. Many Buddhist practitioners have intensively studied their own minds and passed on what they have learned as roadmaps. Mindfulness does not belong to Buddhism, but the modern teachings of mindfulness have been influenced by the practitioners and scholars of the lineage. Consider a useful comparison: coffee originated in Ethiopia and was drunk there for millennia before it made its way to Egypt and the Middle East, and now it fills the cups of drinkers around the world. The effect that coffee has on people is universal and is beloved equally by many Christians, Muslims, and Jews. The effects of mindfulness practices are considerably more mellow than coffee, but they are just as universal. Of course, just as drinking coffee will not make you Ethiopian, practicing mindfulness will not make you Buddhist.

Many of the teachings that are offered in this book have been used for generations by practitioners in the lands of Buddhist culture. As you will see, however, there are no religious connotations in the practices offered here. The practices are a secular offering for you to explore your own awareness, regardless of your religious background. If the practices do not work for you, or seem to conflict with your way of life, there is no pressure to continue with them. Some people love the way coffee affects them, and some hate it. If you like the way mindfulness affects you then it's yours, no membership required. You don't even need to call it mindfulness. You could call it presence, focusing, time-in; you could even call it hop-scotch if that's what your students seem to like. As long as the practices are being taught with integrity, the essence will stay the same.

PART II

✤

Begin with Yourself

Caring for the Caregiver

I lead a significant percentage of any training for teachers as silent mindfulness practice, sitting, walking, and generally withdrawing attention from the busy barrage of outside chatter in service of stillness and inquiry. Whether it is two hours of silence as part of a day long training, or a five-day silent retreat as part of a year-long program, I want teachers to get a direct experience of mindfulness. As you cultivate your own attention and compassion, you will invariably carry this presence into your work with kids. You can offer them the greatest gift of all: simply seeing them through the eyes of compassionate attention.

Susan, a schoolteacher who was a participant of the year-long Mindful Education Institute, walked up anxiously on day two of our silent retreat, asking if we could talk. She and I walked among the oak trees in the California summer sun. "I think that Nancy is really having a hard time," she said about another participant.

"I want to go up and ask if she is okay. It doesn't feel right to just sit there."

"What would it feel like," I asked, "if you let Nancy have her sadness and not make it your job to take that sadness away?"

As I said this Susan's eyes began to well up and she started to cry. "I would feel so sad. Nancy is struggling, my students at home are in such horrible situations, I feel so out of control."

As she cried, I helped orient her into feeling her own emotions instead of focusing so much on the distress of others. I had her imagine bringing all the care and support to her own heart. "In this moment, can you turn all this care toward your own sadness and fear?" Tears rolled down her face as she held her hands to her heart and her appearance seemed to soften.

Susan came to me at the end of the retreat with a deep calmness in her eyes and said that ever since that moment in the trees she had been imagining that she had been cradling her own heart like a baby. "Once we came out of silence, I talked to Nancy and she said she wasn't even sad. I guess I just had so much sadness I was projecting it onto her. It feels so good just to offer myself all the care that I have been giving to everyone else. It's like I'm putting that apple on my desk that I always hoped the kids would give me."

If we are attached to transforming our chaotic classrooms into rooms full of angelic children who line our desks with crisp apples every morning, we are in for a long and frustrating wait. It's great to have a vision of peace and harmony, but we all have to start where we are. We often leap forward, wanting to help our kids relax, forgetting to notice how anxious and in need of relaxation we are. A teacher would never try to lead a math lesson if she didn't know the multiplication tables.

I have had many teachers, therapists, and parents come to me with genuine enthusiasm about mindfulness, asking how they can use it to *save* their kids. When we see the suffering of the children in our world and get a little taste of the mindfulness antidote, our compassionate hearts leap in. "Maybe this can fix everything!" If this is the reason you have bought this book, I applaud you, and then I invite you to slow down and listen a little deeper into your own heart. Whenever someone tells me of their enthusiasm about mindfulness in education I begin by asking, "Do you have your own mindfulness practice?"

In his mindfulness-based stress reduction retreats, Jon Kabat-Zinn often asks, "Why are you here?" He then drops the floor out from under you and asks, "Why are you really here?" And one more time for good measure, "Why are you really, *really* here?" You may truthfully say, "I am here because so many kids have ADHD and mindfulness could help them cultivate their ability to pay attention" or "I want my children to have the inner resources to counteract the violent video games and other noxious media they are assaulted by." These are good honest, answers, but as you ask why you are really, really, *really* reading this book, I invite you to look into your true motives.

How do you want to transform yourself to be a greater conduit to the learning of the youth that have been brought into your care? What is holding you back from embodying the type of person you hope your kids will become? Every time you ask yourself one of these questions, it is a gift to your students, a far greater gift than any information you might offer. Information is imperative in education, but transformation is where maturity, morality, and wisdom come from. When you are on a path of personal growth, you are modeling to your students the true meaning of mindfulness.

To teach mindfulness to kids, we have to do what Susan did. She started with herself. When we pull back all the projections we have on the world and start with ourselves, we are already modeling mindful education.

As a marriage and family therapist, I often have conversations with parents who bring in their sons or daughters, saying "My child is acting out. Can you fix her?" I ask a bit about the parents' relationship and other home life factors. Usually it will become apparent quickly that this child is the "identified patient" of the family, meaning that there is really a systemic issue. Something is going wrong in the larger family dynamic and the "problem" child is the one expressing it. If the parents are having difficulty in their marriage, I usually say, "The best way I can help your child is for the two of you to come in for couple's therapy." Parents are often amazed at how quickly their child's "issues" are resolved once they face the underlying conflicts in their marriage. Once the parental structure is strong, the child can relax and stop sounding the alarm with his or her behaviors. Like families, emotional and behavioral disorders are often exacerbated in schools when we adults are not taking care of ourselves and our interpersonal staff dynamics.

The way of mindful education takes our attention from all the ways we want to change the world and turns our gaze inward. Instead of taking on the immense and impossible task of trying to get the world around us to calm down, we can notice and learn to manage the wild chatter in our own minds. Calming the mind, though not an easy job, is far more doable than getting the world around us to stop. Instead of trying to get the kids on the playground to be more peaceful, we can begin by realizing how anxious the chaos makes us. When we learn to experience our anxiety in our bodies, noticing the tightness and quickened breathing pattern; we can also learn to use a mindfulness practice to relax and take care of ourselves. Then, even if the playground fights and chaos in the class continue (and they will), we can find that still point in the storm. Without needing anything to change, we can be the guiding light our students are drawn toward. Instead of waiting for the world to be peaceful, we can simply relax and let the world find peace around us.

The When, Where, and How of Mindfulness

❋

A mother once brought her son to Mahatma Gandhi, asking him if he could please give the boy a lecture on how bad it was to eat too many sweets. Gandhi replied that she should return in two weeks. When the weeks passed she brought her son back and Gandhi gave an articulate speech about how unhealthy sweets were to the body and the mind. The mother was appreciative, but confused as well. "Why didn't you just tell him this two week ago?" she asked. "Well at that time I was eating too many sweets myself," Gandhi replied.

Like Gandhi, we must walk our talk. You can take off your teacher's cap for the moment and see if you can squeeze into one of those kid-sized desks. It's your turn to be the student and learn some indispensable mindfulness lessons. There is an inner science to the mind that we can explore as we set up personal awareness experiments. Imagine examining yourself under a microscope. As you commit to an attention practice you will probably notice your mind becoming more focused. As you commit to a heartfulness practice you may begin to feel more compassion arising. You can read research articles on how mindfulness effects the brain, but now it is your turn to practice and conduct your own inner science experiment. Don't take my word for it—see how mindfulness works for you.

When

To cultivate a mindfulness practice, it is important to schedule mindful moments into your day. In our busy schedules we may only have 15 minutes to commit to sitting. That's fine. If you have the time and commitment, try sitting for 40 minutes every day or twice a day. You may try sitting in the mornings or the evenings when you won't be distracted. Find the time that works best for you and stick to that time every day. It can be helpful to put your moments into a daily planner and formally schedule your sitting. Especially when we are new to mindfulness, we often need to make a formal commitment to our practice if we want to be able to turn it into a pattern.

When we ask *when* to practice mindfulness, the answer is: always. We set up a schedule for our mindful sitting and walking practice so we can reinforce an attitude of compassionate presence in every moment of our lives. As this presence expands, we can have a continuity of mindful awareness more and more. To cultivate this continual presence, you can also set mindful reminders for yourself throughout the day. Every time the school bell rings, you can take three mindful breaths. Before every class you can remember to send heartfulness to your kids. Every time you notice yourself distracted or dysregulated, you can return to a few mindful breaths. The time is always now.

Where

Find a spot for your mindfulness practice that is quiet and where you will have minimal distractions. You can set up your sitting spot with objects or art that you find calming or special. Even if this space is just in the corner of a room, it can become your home base. You can also set up a special spot in your classroom to practice. This could be as simple as putting a vase of flowers in one corner of the room and remembering to go to this corner a few times a day to sit still and breathe for a few moments. Remember to stop and smell the flowers.

When we ask *where* to practice mindfulness, the answer is: everywhere. Though finding a specific spot is helpful, we only practice so we can play well on the court. One of the best places to practice is in nature. Take a nice walk on the beach, in the mountains, or down a nice tree-lined street. Try picking a few places in your environment that will be mindful reminder spots. If you pick your front door and the steps to your school, then every time you open your door you can mindfully remember to feel the doorknob in your hand, and every time you walk up the school steps you can feel your legs lifting. As you bring your light of awareness throughout every experience of your life, pretty soon your whole world is shining.

How

In this section you will be guided through four mindfulness practices. We will learn to cultivate embodiment, attention, heartfulness, and interconnection. I recommend that you practice at least once a day for a month to see the effects that the practices have on your body, mind, and heart and in your relationship to the world. Commit to sit every day, not as a discipline but as a gift to yourself.

Eventually mindfulness practice can become a home base that we love coming back to, but at first mindfulness sometimes feels like an annoying chore. As much as possible, see of you can look to these periods of time as an opportunity to slow down your mind and drop into your heart. If for nothing else, your mindfulness time can be seen as the one time where you have no responsibilities. No need to respond to your phone, your students, or even your nagging thoughts. This is your time.

When we ask *how* to practice mindfulness, the answer is: however you can. Mindfulness is classically taught in sitting, walking, standing, and lying postures. That covers most of the positions our bodies tend to find themselves in. You can mindfully jog, ski, dance, stand in line, lie in the bathtub, or sit at the coffee shop. Mindfulness can look as many ways as we can. Eventually we can be mindful in every action and posture, but to strengthen this capacity we begin with sitting and walking practices.

For the mindful attention, heartfulness, and interconnection lessons you will be in a sitting posture. It's important to remember to be both relaxed and focused in your posture. Remember to sit up straight, with a sense of nobility, as if you were a king or queen. Simultaneously let your body rest down into the earth. Depending on what's comfortable for you, you can sit on the ground, in a chair, or if necessary lie down.

Whatever posture you use, remember the two indispensable legs of mindfulness: focus and relaxation. The first leg of our mindfulness practice is our *focused attention*. With mindfulness practices we hone our attention, anchoring ourselves to our direct awareness in the present moment. As we commit to our mindfulness practice, our attention muscles grow stronger. However, if we only have our focus leg, we may find ourselves getting too stressed and perfection oriented.

This is where the second leg of mindfulness comes to the rescue—relaxation. *Mindful relaxation* opens the way for nonjudgment, compassion, and going with the flow. In our mindfulness practice we learn to welcome whatever arises; happiness, sadness, pain, pleasure, blue skies, and rain. We let the river take us and accept ourselves, and the world, exactly as we are.

Of course, if we were only going with the flow we may have some trouble getting our lesson plans finished, but our first leg, our dedicated focus, can help us avoid missing the many very real commitments in our lives. Here is a quick exercise to help you connect to your two legs of mindfulness.

Focused and Relaxed Exercise

As you read these words, wherever you are, notice the weight of your body and your contact with the earth beneath you. Whatever tasks you have, whatever worries from the past or for the future, just for this moment, let your entire body melt. On the next exhale, let your whole body relax as if it's resting into a warm bath. On the next inhale, focus your attention and let your spine straighten. With a dedicated focus, notice your breath and your body rising tall. You can relax on every exhale and then focus on every inhale.

Try breathing like this for a few minutes, upright on the inhale and letting go on the exhale. Now sit for a few minutes feeling your body upright and relaxed at the same time. See if you can be completely focused while simultaneously being totally relaxed. Your muscles can soften while your awareness is focused on every breath.

Try returning to this practice as many times as possible throughout the day. You can do a version of this while you are speaking in front of a class. Simply concentrate on feeling your feet on the ground, letting your body relax and simultaneously focusing your senses. We educators know that our finest teaching happens with a balance of prepared focus and creative flow.

Cultivating Embodiment

In one third-grade classroom, I received a very clear lesson on the need to begin mindfulness with embodiment. After weeks of lessons, we had reached a point where I would walk into the classroom, ring a bell, and immediately we would enter five minutes of silent, mindful breathing. When I first started working with the students they had been very distracted, but as the lessons went on they had become connected to the practices and started taking them seriously. One day, after four or five weeks of working together, we were sitting and breathing for a minute when I started hearing some crinkling and looked up to see a student fidgeting with her books and papers. I could tell the noises were affecting other students, and my own anxiousness began to build in my throat. Then, as I watched, her fiddling fingers knocked a box of paperclips from her desk to the linoleum floor, where it exploded with clinking sounds.

Of course all the other students looked up, and as I was about to tell them to focus in again, I realized that I was trying to control the shaky energy in the room and contain my own anxiousness. My heart opened up, and I realized there was a palpable tension in the room that this girl was expressing and the rest of us were feeling. I turned to the girl and said, "I notice that you are moving around a bunch. In the past you have been very still for our mindful breathing sessions. What is the difference today? Do you need anything?" Without missing a beat she said, "I'm having trouble sitting still. Can we do that shake-still exercise again?"

In an earlier session, when the class had been rather boisterous, I had done a practice with them where we shook our bodies and then got totally still, shook our bodies and then got still, over and over. The last thing I want to do is bottle the natural energy inside children. I like to let students shake if they need to shake and express anger if they need to express anger. Whatever is true in the body can be honored and expressed in a healthy way.

"That sounds like a great idea," I said. "Let's shake our bodies and get still and then we can do our mindful breathing afterward." We did the shake-still exercise a few times and then sat through a five-minute silent breathing practice with a sense of being really settled. This student knew far better than I did in that moment what the whole class needed. She knew that her energetic system was not ready to be still, and she needed to connect to her body before doing anything else. In the same way, the anxiousness I noticed in my body was a cue to explore the frenetic energy in the room that I was picking up on. Every experience has information if we listen closely enough. When I was curious about my own anxiousness and remembered to listen to my student's experience, I was able to let go of my fixed plan and open to what was truly needed in the moment.

There is a great storehouse of wisdom in our bodies from which we are often disconnected. Our bodies are our vehicles in this life, not just to get our brains from on place to another but the means through which we come into contact with the world. Our bodies are where we feel our emotions, where we have our thoughts; they are the places that every experience happens. Our senses are here to give us information. A common confusion in practicing mindfulness is in thinking that the goal is to transcend the difficulties of our human bodies. This is not the case. There is great merit in learning to befriend and come home to our bodies, even if the back is hurting, the heart is grieving, or there are any assortment of annoying sensory phenomena. In fact, bringing our awareness to the difficult feelings inside gives us the knowledge we need to learn and heal.

Some of the best ways to develop embodiment are the simplest. Take a walk in the park, go surfing, dance, or garden; basically, do whatever you enjoy doing, but with a deepened awareness of your body. Other practices that can serve amazingly well are yoga, tai chi, aikido, and other martial and movement arts. Many of these practices have a direct focus on cultivating awareness in the body, often with breath as a key component.

Embodiment Practice: Mindful Walking

Preparation

To begin, find a quiet place where you will not be too distracted. This can be indoors or outside in nature. Choose a short distance, possibly 10 steps, and let this be the court on which you practice your mindful walking. When we practice mindful walking, the destination is here and the goal is now.

Exercise

Notice the way gravity is delicately tethering you to the Earth. Notice what sensations are in your body, what emotions are alive within you, and what state your mind is in.

When you start to walk, take very slow steps so that you can fully feel the movements of your body. Bring attention to your feet rising and falling, compressing against the ground and lifting into the air. The more curious you get about the movement, the more keenly you can witness how each step tilts your hips, shoulders, and head and how every single part of the body is balancing, flexing, relaxing, and contributing to the forward motion.

Take about 10 steps before you stop, then take a moment to feel your breath in your body, turn around mindfully, and walk back the 10 steps. As you see, we are not going anywhere. Instead of trying to get somewhere else, with each step we are practicing arriving, arriving, arriving in the present moment.

Postexercise Reflection

You may get to the end of the 10 steps and realize you've been thinking about taxes the entire time. Don't beat yourself up. Notice the way the mind is always trying to busy itself with something other than what is happening right now, and once you have gained this awareness, gently return to the sensations of the body as it moves. You could even say to yourself, "Once again I have been lost in distraction, thank you for another opportunity to come back to my body, to my heart, to the present moment." Remember, a compassionate attitude is what you want to bring to the whole process.

Additional Notes and Advice

- It can be wonderful to practice mindful walking out in the world. You can take a long walk in nature and feel the wind, hear the sounds of birds, and see the colors of the world around you. Remember not to rush. Allow yourself time to receive all of the communications the environment is sending you.

- If you have a disability or injury that makes it hard for you to walk, this practice is easily done without putting one foot in front of the other. One can slowly feel one's hands moving a wheelchair or even slowly feeling the arms rise and fall. The point is to cultivate attention in the body and in the direct environment, not to get from here to there.

- Other examples of embodiment practices are qigong, yoga, Pilates, dance, or any physical activity where attention is brought to the sensory field. Some practitioners find mindful walking an easier gateway to mindfulness because sitting still feels too uncomfortable for them at first. If this is the case, then you can always practice mindful walking instead of sitting. On breaks between classes, or any moment when you have 15 minutes, you can take some time to drop out of your spinning thoughts and anchor yourself in your body with some mindful movement.

Cultivating Attention

※

We can focus with our eyes, our ears, our sense of touch, our breathing, our tasting—we can even focus on the nature of thinking itself. If you can experience it, you can focus on it. Whichever phenomenon we chose to anchor our awareness on, the practice is basically the same. We anchor the mind on one field of experience and then watch the waves that distract us, pulling us this way and that. Then we let the anchor draw us back to the object of our attention. When we notice our distraction, we notice it gently, without beating ourselves up, simply taking it as another chance to be fully present.

You can use metaphors to help yourself avoid getting distracted, such as watching passing clouds or not getting on a train that is pulling up. I have taught mindful attention practices to many high school sport teams. With baseball teams I will say, "As you are focusing mindfully on your breath, you can be aware of a thought passing like a pitch that's outside the strike zone. You may notice a desire to swing, but just let the thought go by and keep focusing on the breath." When working with little children, I often have them close their eyes and try to catch their butterfly thoughts with a net.

As we explore our capacity to stabilize our minds, it is of great value to diligently focus but not be too hard on ourselves. Many of us have a strict inner schoolteacher who will rap us on the knuckles if we're not doing something just right. Our inner schoolteacher plays a valuable role in helping harness our attention, but just as we are learning to teach our children compassionately, we must be compassionate with ourselves.

Our minds, especially in today's modern media-filled culture, are swirling with thoughts. When we sit down for just a minute we can experience what feels like a flood of unstoppable mind stuff.

Mindfulness helps us cultivate the balance, patience, and attention we need to wade through the muck of mind chaos. We open our attention nonjudgmentally and watch all the thoughts, emotions, and sensations pass by us like we are sitting on a rock in a stream and the gurgling water is flowing by all around us.

As we build our attention muscles, we can gain a vigilance that allows us to become less frequently and less severely caught in the currents of judgmental and fearful thoughts. As we cultivate our stabilized presence, we build neural connections limiting our reactivity and expanding our capacity to keep our hearts open to every flowing phenomenon. Without getting lost in the waves, we learn to stay anchored and navigate skillfully.

Attention Practice: Mindful Breathing

Preparation

Begin by sitting in a posture that embodies upright nobility and relaxed kindness. Feel your body sitting tall and straight while letting the muscles melt.

Exercise

In your upright seated posture, bring your awareness to the sensations of your breath in your belly. With an attentive interest, see what the in-breath and out-breath feel like.

Let the breath come in and out naturally without trying to alter it in any way. Notice if the breath is shallow or deep, tight or relaxed, short or long. Let the breath be however it is; if it is shallow let it be shallow, if the breath is tight, bring your kind attention to the sensations of tightness.

As you notice the particulars of the breath, see if you can maintain your upright attention and your relaxed sense of letting things be exactly as they are.

The mind invariably will wander away; once you notice that the mind has wandered, you can return to the sensations of the breath. There is no use beating yourself up for wandering away. The fact that you have noticed the mind wandering means you are already paying attention, which is good news, because then you can return to the breath.

Keep the attention on the sensations in the breath. See if you can cultivate an intimacy with the breath, enjoying the flow of sensations swirling in and out of the body. Notice the subtleties of the circuit of breath. Let the breath become a thread you hold onto as you follow the unfolding experience of the present moment.

Postexercise Reflection

As we practice mindfulness, we are looking into the mirror at our own minds. We may see an agitated mind, a calm mind, or whatever mind state we currently inhabit. The point of mindfulness is not to get rid of our thoughts or create a state of total bliss. The intention behind a mindfulness practice is to realize what is true. So if your mind is full of thoughts and your heart is aching, then in the eyes of mindfulness you are completely successful if you spend your entire sitting practice simply witnessing all the agitation. Instead of needing a particular state of mind to be happy, we can simply be really nice to ourselves and accept our minds exactly as they are.

Cultivating Heartfulness

Our intention with heartfulness is to cultivate a compassionate presence, the type of unconditional open-heartedness we feel toward a beautiful baby. Then we learn to extend this compassion toward ourselves and all other beings, even the annoying ones. It's easy to feel love and care toward a giggling, beaming baby, but quite a practice to keep our hearts open and compassionate toward a child having a tantrum.

The way that we extend our reach of compassion is by learning to be ever more compassionate to ourselves. Sometimes when we look into our own hearts it's like there's a happy baby in there, and at other times there is a child in full tantrum mode. With heartfulness practices we learn to support the happiness, kindness, gratitude, and other beneficial qualities we find inside while bringing a kind attention to difficult emotions such as anger, jealousy, fear, and sadness.

When little children are asked to send kind thoughts to themselves, they happily give themselves a big hug and wish for their own happiness, safety, health, and peacefulness. They don't say, "I don't know if I deserve all this kindness," or "Isn't there someone else more deserving than me?" They just smile and send themselves kind thoughts. When asked what else they might wish, they will often say things like "May it be my birthday every day" or "May nobody ever be mean." Most little children have not yet learned to protect their hearts.

Heartfulness begins with the radical practice of remembering how to open our hearts as easily as we did when we were in kindergarten. By the time we grow up we've built many layers of emotional armor. We've done so for very good reasons at the time; we were protecting ourselves from the harsh realities of the world. Unfortunately, when we armor our hearts, we limit our capacity to give and receive love, and we feel disconnected from ourselves.

When I teach teenagers heartfulness, I realize that many of them often think it's cheesy or lame. Whenever I encounter this, I talk to the students about how sad I think it is that we think it's cool to be mean to each other and put each other down. I ask them, "Why do you think being kind and vulnerable isn't cool? Since all of us want to be liked and to have others like us, why is kindness cheesy? Doesn't putting each other down to get people to like us seem like a poor strategy?"

This conversation always opens up an intriguing discussion. After we have gotten honest with each other about how we want to be accepted for who we really are, I ask, "Who wants to get cheesy with me now?" I find teenagers to be intrigued and excited by this conversation. This opens a path for students to understand the power of vulnerability. I find that when students have the bravery to share an authentic part of themselves, it relaxes the whole room. Everyone wants to be able to open up their armor and share what is true in their hearts. One student shares, and then the rest follow like an avalanche. Vulnerability is then seen as a courageous act to be respected instead of judged or picked on.

As teachers and child care providers, many of us know so well how to care for others, but we have often forgotten how to care for ourselves. We may tell children to be nice to each other, but when we look into our own minds we see how cruel we are to ourselves. We are perpetually judging ourselves, comparing ourselves to others, and putting ourselves down. To be truly compassionate to others, you need to care for the person who deserves your love and care the most: you. You don't need to go far to find this compassion. You can simply take the genuine caring you have for kids and send it in toward yourself.

The following heartfulness practice draws on this genuine strength of yours: your compassion for your students. You can learn to turn the light of compassion in on yourself. As we begin to cultivate self-compassion, we may hit up against our own self-judgments, feelings of shame, and self-limiting beliefs. Instead of trying to get rid of our difficult emotions, we bring the light of our compassion to melt our inner armoring. We learn to hold the crying and tantrumming child within ourselves. With an integrated emotional self we can bring our compassion, forgiveness, and kindness into the world. We embody compassion, loving the world as it is, without trying to change it.

Heartfulness Practice: Caring Phrases

Preparation

Find a comfortable seated position where your body can fully relax.

Exercise

Bring your attention to your chest and heart. See what feelings, emotions, and sensations you find there. Without trying to experience anything specific, locate your awareness in your heart.

When you feel relaxed and focused, picture a child you care about, one who evokes kind feelings. Imagine this child in your mind's eye and see what your heart feels like. You may notice happiness, compassion, tenderness, or any other sympathetic emotions.

Now offer the following wishes to this child either silently or out loud and keep your attention on the feeling in your heart.

- May you be happy
- May you be safe
- May you be healthy
- May you be peaceful

Offering the wishes at least a few more times, continue to be aware of your heart.

Now shift your heartfulness gaze toward yourself. With the same kindness you sent to the child, send these heartfulness wishes to yourself, and as you do so, note how this affects your body.

- May I be happy
- May I be safe
- May I be healthy
- May I be peaceful

When you are ready, bring your attention back to the sensations in your heart for a few more breaths, this time without saying the phrases. Simply sit and notice. When you are ready, gently open your eyes.

Postexercise Reflections

We began this heartfulness practice by picturing a child for whom it was easy to feel care and love. We don't need to do much to open our hearts—we can simply picture an adorable child and our hearts respond sympathetically. Once we have opened our hearts, we can turn the spotlight of care inward and send ourselves the same kind acceptance. This can be like a healing balm to our hearts.

When we send ourselves kindness, it is like we are recharging our heart batteries. We can much more easily send our heartfulness out to others from this place of emotional fullness. We can picture all of our students before they come into class and send kind thoughts to each one. The graduate-level heartfulness is learning to send kind thoughts to colleagues, students, and family members who annoy us, or even those against whom we hold a serious grudge. As we open our circle of compassion, we can learn to forgive and understand the suffering of others.

Cultivating Interconnectedness

✺

At the 1940 scientific meeting of the British Psycho-analytical Society, the eminent psychologist Donald Winnicott shocked the psychoanalytic community by stating, "There is no such thing as an infant." Any parent might reasonably ask, "What is this thing that I have to feed 20 times a day then?" Winnicott was making the point that a baby never exists outside of the context of the caretaker. In a healthy caregiver–newborn relationship, a form of symbiosis occurs. The two become an indivisible unit. You could say a mother doesn't exist either, for a mother never exists outside of the context of a child. Similarly, a student doesn't exist without a teacher, or a teacher without a student.

If we open our view we see that a human being doesn't exist either. No one has ever existed without the sun, without water, without the trees that exhale the oxygen we breath. Every being is indivisibly dependent on other beings. This consciousness—the consciousness of interdependence—can transform our way of being in the world.

Science, when looked at closely, offers a far more profound explanation of existence than any fiction writer could ever imagine. At one time, arising out of pure emptiness, a big bang occurred, scattering energy into nearly infinite space. The building blocks that now form everything from stones to human brains are made from the same atomic soup. In fields ranging from molecular biology to astrophysics, modern science is continually discovering how miraculously interconnected everything is. From the great gears of the universe turning in tandem to molecules in our bodies swirling in a perfect symbiosis, we have proof everywhere of the underlying interdependence of all things.

With an investigative eye, you will notice this interconnection. Simply sit quietly in nature and bring your open interest to what is happening all around you. If you listen closely enough, it is as if the whole world is waking up, the wind tumbling through the trees, the trill call of the sparrow, the great variety of subtle buzzes in the ear. When you spend some time listening, you may just realize that the world has been awake this whole time and it's you who have been asleep, distracted, caught up in the drama of the mind. It doesn't matter when you stop or when you remember, your breath is right here waiting for you. The world all around and inside of you is calling to you, inviting you to join the celebration.

Interconnectedness Practice: Listening Outside and Inside

Preparation

Sit comfortably and upright in a calm setting, letting your eyes close.

Exercise

Bring your awareness to your breath, following the sensations in your belly on the inhale and exhale. Follow this for a few minutes, and every time your mind wanders off returning to the awareness of the breath.

Shift your awareness to the outside world by mindfully listening to sounds. Let the sounds arrive at the shores of your ears, noticing the beginning and end of each noise. Continue listening for a few minutes with a focused interest. Every time you get caught in thoughts, return to the sounds. Notice how you are in a field of sounds arising and passing away.

Now, return to listening to your inner world by feeling your breath again. For a few minutes listen to the inner sensations of your body as you breathe in and out.

One more time, switch to listening to the outside sounds for a few minutes. Open your awareness to distant sounds as well as little noises in your own body.

Now notice every type of phenomenon inside and outside: thoughts, sensations, sounds, smells, emotions. Instead of focusing on one sense perception, you can open your awareness to all senses simultaneously.

When you are ready, let your eyes open and take in the sights of the world with the same vast presence. See if you can take this open presence with you into your day.

Postexercise Reflection

Through this practice we shuttled our awareness from our inside world to our outside world and noticed all of our senses simultaneously. This practice supports us in becoming aware of the relationship between our inner and outer worlds. With this practice we can see how external influences affect our inner state of being as well as how our inner state of being effects how we act and relate with others.

We begin mindfulness practice on the inside, learning to relax in our bodies, focus our minds, and take care of our hearts. Once we have done this we can learn to use interconnection practices to bring the compassionate awareness we cultivated into the world.

Cultivating Emotional Intelligence

❋

To teach, parent, or even develop a close relationship with another person, a certain level of emotional maturity is indispensable. Many of our actions (we could even say most) are created by unconscious motives. We have underlying drives within ourselves that we are not aware of. Whether or not we are conscious of them, they motivate many of our behaviors, especially our actions in relationship to others. Imagine your inner world as a classroom of students. There are all these inner parts: the inner class clown, the inner teachers' pet, the inner straight-A student, the inner rebel. If we don't recognize each of our inner parts and learn to meet their needs, then the inner class is always in conflict. First we must learn to create a mindful and accepting teacher in our own minds, someone who can track and care for our inner classroom. Only then can we embody the compassionate teacher we want to become.

All of our inner parts are natural expressions of who we authentically are. Babies are unapologetically blissful at one moment and enraged in the next. The emotional waves of childhood flow unimpeded until they bump into the parent's and teacher's fears and insecurities. Our primary caregivers and teachers trained us through their very being in how to relate to our inner classroom. They learned from their teachers and parents in which parts were acceptable and which were not, and they passed these messages on to us. Then the child splits, realizing that to receive love, one's authentic expression needs to be muted or morphed. This is the birth of *suppression*, the process in which we hide our authentic selves from the world and strategize a persona to get our basic needs met. As an organism we decide it's safer to be loved for a false self than unloved for an authentic one. If we get sent to the principal for being too silly and energetic, our class clown part learns that it is not accepted, and we develop a self-critic, the stern inner principal, who tells us this jovial exuberant part is not allowed and needs to be censored.

One of the inevitable byproducts of suppression is an unconscious strategy called *projection*. To understand projections, simply think of the wonderful days when you walk into your classroom, having had a cheerful morning, and find all the students are smiling and any annoyances just roll off you. Other times, when you are feeling dragged down by the weight of the world, you walk into class and all the students seem to be intentionally getting on your nerves, your colleagues are being inconsiderate, and all the kids in the hall are "little monsters!" Our inner angst paints the world with a dark hue, not the rose-colored glasses of our happy days. If you have never explored the phenomenon of projection it may seem odd, but once you look you will realize that, as Anaïs Nin said, "We don't see things as they are, we see them as we are."

Particularly, we project onto the outside when we are uncomfortable with our experience on the inside. Many of us grew up in a family where our parents told us that they would love us when we were nice and not when we were angry. If you express anger, the message went, you have to go to your room. In other words, if you express the angry part of yourself, love will be withdrawn. In these circumstances we learn, very intelligently, to suppress our anger to receive the love and affection we need as nourishment to grow into healthy human beings.

Sigmund Freud, the father of psychoanalysis, is acknowledged as having said, "Unexpressed emotions will never die. They are buried alive and will come forth later in uglier ways." The inner parts of ourselves that we don't accept and keep sending to the inner principal's office have been labeled troublemakers, but the more we try to get rid of them, the more they act out. Our inner world insists on being experienced. If we are perpetually trying to escape from painful or unpleasant experiences, we'll often find ourselves seeing those painful experiences mirrored in the people and world around us. They sneak out and project onto the world so we can relate to them as if they belong to someone else. We project out what we find too painful to accept inside.

It is crucial for child care providers to be aware of these projections. Let's say you have an early morning argument with your significant other. You show up at school and even though you are feeling shaky and irritated, you decide to put on a happy face for your students and try to suppress your emotions. This may work for a little while, but there is a low-level irritation that you can feel every time a student drops something on the floor or takes a little too long to understand the material. It would be easy in this situation to project onto a student that they are intentionally trying to annoy you. The truth, however, is probably that the students are having their own difficult emotional experience that they don't know how to deal with.

This is where our mindfulness practice comes in. When the class won't settle down and we find ourselves slipping into negative projections, we can learn to feel the emotions in our bodies as sensations. Instead of circulating in our frustrating thoughts we can drop down into our bodies and figure out what scripted, learned responses the chaos in the classroom is bringing up for us.

Mindfulness offers us the skill of witnessing our frenzied thoughts without getting swept up in them. Whenever you notice your mind in a hamster wheel of difficult thoughts, you can bet that there is an emotion somewhere in your body that your brain is trying to get rid of by thinking its way out of it. If you are ruminating about the morning argument you had, you may be trying to come up with the perfect counter-argument so that you will be understood. The real reason we ruminate is that there is some distressing emotion like anger or sadness inside and we are trying to figure out a perfect strategy that can shift our experience.

The next time you find your mind in the spinning, do a scan of your body and see where the tension or emotion is. This physical experience is a direct palpable place that you can bring your kind attention and relaxing breath. Instead of trying to think your way out of it, see if you can feel your way into it. Instead of trying to come up with the perfect argument to get someone to understand you, in this moment you can develop understanding and care for your own distressed heart.

When you anchor your attention on feeling the sensations in your body instead of getting lost in angry or jealous thoughts, you are "pulling back your projections." Pulling back projections creates an inner responsibility where we *own* our emotions. We can learn to care for all of our inner parts, making space for every character in the inner classroom. You may find a part inside that feels like a three-year-old throwing a tantrum. Instead of trying to shut this part up or blame someone else, you can learn to care for this part with genuine self-compassion.

When we pull back our projections and own our emotions, we see the world as it is rather than as we've imagined it to be. When we do this we cultivate what's called *discernment*. The classroom is driving you crazy, so you take a moment to notice what is happening inside. You realize you had an argument with your spouse that morning and have been feeling on edge all day. Notice where the tension is in your body, breathe into the uncomfortable feeling, and let your body relax on the exhale. Aware of your own feelings, you gain the discernment necessary to look up at your students and see them as they are, rather than coloring them and their actions with your frustration. Discernment allows us to see which parts of our experience are projection and which are true experiences. As we begin to more fully inhabit ourselves, we shed the need to project so much and are therefore able to act more consciously in our relationships.

One clear sign that you are progressing on this path is if you notice less drama arising in your life. Of course mindfulness cannot stop tragedies from occurring, but as these phenomena arise, we may notice ourselves responding without as much personal affront. If a tree were to fall in your path, you wouldn't imagine that the tree fell because it didn't like you. You know how to depersonalize that event; similarly, you may see the same disruptive behaviors of students, and somehow they're not sticking to you, not being personalized. You're able to handle the day with humor and grace.

I've said it before, and I'll say it again: one of the amazing benefits of starting to practice mindfulness is that your world will seem to transform around you. In my year-long teacher training we begin with a week of silent retreat and then months of inner work and personal practice. After months of this inner work, without any discussion of how to deliver these practices to children, I ask participants how their classrooms have changed. Emails inevitably pour in describing transformations of students and classrooms without a single intervention having been offered to the students. The changes came as a by-product of the teachers' work on themselves.

Children are incredibly attuned to teachers and rely on us to help them self-regulate. Any sports coach knows how their encouragement can help a frustrated player. Our children look to the sidelines to see how they are doing in our eyes. When a child feels truly seen, when they feel that their teacher is really interested in them as a human being, they can realize their own worth. Not only does this make them better students, it helps them gain lasting self-esteem and self-compassion.

It is our own attention, inspiration, and happiness that lays the foundation for our children to cultivate their own healthy way of being in the world. As our hearts expand, we invite students to open up, relax, and let their creative authenticity blossom.

Pulling Back Projection Practice: The Projection Journal

Preparation

In this practice we will learn how to witness our judgments, pull back our projections, and work with our emotions. To do this you will need a *projection journal*. Carry this journal around with you and whenever you notice yourself judging someone, being jealous, or having any intense hamster wheel thoughts about someone else, write down the words that are going through your head. For example, when you witness yourself thinking, "that student is so annoying," write down the words, "That student is so annoying."

You will need about five minutes to go through the journaling process. If you don't have time for the whole exercise when the projection thought goes through your head, simply write the thought down in shorthand and finish the process later.

Exercise

When you notice a judgment moving through your mind jot it down in your projection journal.

Notice which emotions are connected to the thought you've written down. Anger, sadness, fear, or any others. Write down a list of whichever emotions you find.

Which physical sensations reside within these emotions? Do you notice tightness, shakiness, heat, cold, or any other specific sensations? For example, sadness may be made of tightness in the throat and heaviness of heart.

Even if the emotions and sensations are really uncomfortable, you can spend a few moments simply feeling them without trying to push them away. Imagine the sensations and emotions are a crying child you hold in your arms. For a few moments with every inhale kindly hold your emotions and then with every exhale you can let your whole body relax. Try this relaxing breath for a minute.

When you have finished, scan through your body again and write down a list of what emotions and sensations you notice now.

Cultivating Mindful
Communication

✳

As we practice mindfulness, we can gain a greater understanding of who we are beneath our everyday personality and posturing. We can relax into ourselves without needing to be anything for anyone. Our cultivation of this authentic presence is tested, however, when we enter into contact with others. You may find that you complete your mindfulness practice feeling a great sense of equanimity and inner stillness, and then one word from your partner or an argument between two students can completely set you off. It is of the utmost importance to learn how to be actively mindful in our relationships with others, especially when we are the models for the children in our care.

Humans are relational creatures by nature. From infancy we learn to attach to our caregivers and create bonds in which we feel safe and secure. From early on we scan our environments and learn which behaviors and expressions are acceptable. We learn the politics of interpersonal connection before we even learn to speak.

When we examine our behaviors as adults, we will see that these early interactional blueprints still govern the ways we navigate relationships. We may make an insecure smile even though we feel sad, laugh even though we are nervous, cry when we are angry, or puff our bodies up when we actually feel scared and disempowered. Through mindfulness, we can begin to witness how much of our behavior is motivated by trying to please others and protect ourselves.

Mindful communication begins with grounding ourselves in our own authentic presence. We can see what happens when we allow ourselves to be exactly who we are in the present moment without covering up with our usual masks and stories. When we try this, it often brings up some discomfort. We have built up our personality fortresses during times in the past when we were let down or attacked for being our authentic selves. Opening our gates can leave us feeling very vulnerable, and if we do not do it with care and discernment, it can be rewounding. We need friends and community members with whom we can learn to speak and relate in a new way.

We all have basic needs for happiness, connection, and meaning, and we are looking to get those needs met. These are universal needs, and we want to honor them. But our strategies for getting these needs met are where we often get into trouble. We might try to get love by being mean, or hide our true feelings about something because we want to feel safe. These strategies may have worked at earlier moments in our lives, but now that we have internalized them we may find ourselves like a fly knocking against a windowpane over and over again. We need to consider whether there is a better way to get this need met.

Mike Rice, the head coach of the Rutgers University men's basketball program, was fired when a video emerged of him shoving, throwing basketballs, and taunting his players. After Rice had been universally denounced for his behaviors, the head of the Positive Coaching Alliance, Jim Thompson, said, "I am happy the media understands how terrible these behaviors are, but what they are not saying is how poor a strategy this belittling and abusive behavior is. Not only is it wrong, it's just bad coaching and it doesn't get the results you want."For generations sports teams learned to haze their young students and give tough love to make their players fierce competitors. These strategies were not used because they were effective, but because that was what had been modeled by the proceeding generations of coaches. What we're learning now is that positive coaching is not only emotionally supportive, it's successful. Mindful communication is not just a nice thing to do, it's effective.

Mindful communication helps us deconstruct old, harmful communication patterns. We can learn to observe our underlying intentions and then gain clarity on the effect of our actions on others. For example, our intention may be to help empower our students, but the effect may very well be disempowering. With mindfulness, we can become communication scientists. We can see how our statements and behaviors actually affect our students.

Learn to listen deeply to your students and your colleagues. We support our students by communicating with them, learning from them what their needs are and which strategies best meet those needs. As we cultivate our mindful listening skills, interpersonal understanding naturally arises. Being understood and seen is a deep form of nourishment for everyone. As you learn to truly listen, you'll be better equipped to seek out relationships and communities that will meet your need to be seen and heard. Try to pay close attention to how different relationships, settings, and situations affect you, and seek out experiences where you feel accepted, respected, and loved.

Mindful Communication Practice: Stop, Reflect, Speak from the Heart

Preparation

The next time you find yourself in a disagreement, see if you can stop for a moment and reflect. Use this process to be able to listen and respond in a mindful way.

Exercise

Take some time to feel how your body is being affected by the conflict. Are you feeling angry, sad, tense, or ungrounded?

Feel the weight in the bottom of your feet, let your body relax, feel yourself rooted to the Earth.

Notice your breath coming in and out, feeling any tension on the inhale and relaxing on the exhale.

Try to recognize that you may be entrenched in your own sense of rightness. This is natural, and all of us get caught like this, but see if you can let go of your perspective for a moment.

Even if thoughts are flying through your head while the other person is talking, see if you can really listen and receive their words without letting your own thoughts get in the way.

Instead of planning what you are going to say while the other person is speaking, see if you can notice how your heart is affected by what the person is saying. When they are done speaking, take a few mindful breaths and notice how your body and heart feel. Don't give advice or judgments. Speak in "I" statements about what is happening inside of you. When you speak see if you can share directly from your heart.

Postexercise Reflection

One of the most necessary skills in mindful communication practice is willingness to be wrong. You may realize that a totally well-intentioned teaching strategy you have had for years has been having the opposite effect. Instead of beating yourself up for this, see it as an opportunity to change your strategy. Instead of operating from assumptions, you can learn to operate from direct experience.

Mindfulness in Our
Modern World

※

In my psychotherapy practice I see the accelerating speed of technology and media reflected in my clients' nervous systems. Sam, a 13-year-old client, spent the first few months of our sessions rapidly talking about the video game Zelda. At first I tried to get him to talk about his family, school, anything but Zelda, but then I let go and tried to get as interested as I could in this world he was so immersed in.

After a few months of hour-long downloads about magic swords and scary dungeons, the work spontaneously shifted. Sam walked into our sessions and looked me straight in the eyes for the first time, and said, "I know that I'm hiding from everything by playing the video games. But what else is there? Everyone at school makes fun of me, my parents argue all the time, my brother never wants to hang out, what am I supposed to do?" I was deeply affected by this, and Sam cried as he spoke about his feeling of isolation. From then on he would regularly come in and spend the whole session pouring out his feelings about his parents and what was going on at school. Sam realized the only place in his life he had felt empowered, connected, and happy had been in the video game. He was learning to face his difficult emotions, share them, and feel empowered through his vulnerability.

Many of us have our own forms of Sam's experience. We have basic needs for connection, fun, and meaning, but when we lack these experiences in our lives we may look for them online, in our phones, or on the television. Although there is a time and place for these things, they are often unable to offer true satisfaction of the deeper nourishment we really want. Learning to slow down and reconnect to our bodies and hearts can feel like a radical act. Some Japanese monks have a practice of sitting down in the middle of a bustling street corner as throngs of chatting people and beeping cars and bikes go by them. Their practice is to find incorruptible stillness amid the din of mechanized life. Instead of escaping into the monastery, they sit in the full current of the stream, demonstrating to all of us that there is another way. There is a stillness within us that is possible even with the beeping text alerts, homework assignments, and teacher meetings. You can ask yourself in this moment, "Is the stillness I seek not already here?"

If you look deep inside you will find that the stillness you most seek is already with you. But there is also probably a whole lot of chaos in there as well. One immediate experience we may notice as we begin a mindfulness practice is how frenzied our minds can be and how uncomfortable our emotions and bodies are. Our bodies may feel fidgety, and our eyes may want to look at the clock every minute to see when the practice will end. It's like we are pulling the emergency break on a train and it slowly comes to a halt, screeching and grinding the whole way. As we stop and look inside, we see all the feelings that we have been neglecting and turning away from.

Think of yourself as a plant that may need more or less water, sun, or fertilizer. We wouldn't blame a plant for wilting if it wasn't being watered, and we can't blame ourselves for feeling emotionally drained if we have not been nourishing ourselves and have been sitting in rooms with harsh fluorescent lights and poor circulation. Maybe you need to spend more time outside with friends or cut down on work. Generally we are healthier with less stress and more time in authentic connections with friends and in a natural environment.

At home, my wife and I have a 6 pm Internet curfew for ourselves. I rarely eat refined sugar or drink alcohol, and I have learned, sadly, that eating dairy disturbs my digestion. I have had to let go of many things as I become more conscious of how different experiences affect me. I call this the "curse of consciousness." The more conscious you become, the better you will know how things affect you. The down side of this is you may find, like me, that you can never eat ice cream again. That is sad, but the path of truly taking care of myself has opened a door of inner connectedness and health that I wouldn't give up for all the ice cream sundaes in the world. This path of mindfulness can be revolutionary.

To locate ourselves, we may need to swim against the stream of distraction. We can bravely do what Sam did when he admitted how he was trying to get his needs met through a video game because his life was so unsatisfying. He didn't quit playing Zelda, as we don't have to quit all of our enjoyments, but he did get in touch with his sense of dissatisfaction and learned to get his needs met in some nongame ways as well.

Remember the great paradox: when we face our vulnerability and stress, we can learn to take care of ourselves better and be more authentic in the world. We can't do this alone. We need to enlist support for our effort and cultivate conditions in which our awareness and connectedness can thrive.

A good way to begin this process is to explore the effects that different friends, places, and situations have on you.

- Notice how you are feeling before and after you watch television.
- Notice how you feel before and after a staff meeting.
- Notice what it feels like to walk out in nature and what it feels like to sit in a windowless room.
- Notice how the food you eat affects your body and mind.

These experiments can help prepare you to be able to make conscious decisions about how best to create supportive conditions in your life. This can be a scary undertaking. When we take the time to slow down and notice things, we may have to admit to ourselves that things need to change. You may realize your classroom is dark and depressing and needs a tune-up. You may realize you are putting all your energy into relationships that are emotionally draining while neglecting other friends and activities that make you happy. Please don't make any life-changing decisions right away. First, just notice how you are being affected.

Through this section we have learned to take care of ourselves and cultivate our own mindfulness practice, and what we need to embody our practice in the world. Once we cultivate a positive inner classroom, we can move on to the practical knowledge of offering these skills to our students. Our students grow healthy and strong much the same way we do. Remember as we move through this book that the foundation for teaching mindfully is always our own mindfulness practice.

PART III

❀

The Mindful Classroom

A teacher's major contribution may pop out anonymously in the life of some ex-student's grandchild. A teacher, finally, has nothing to go on but faith, a student nothing to offer in return but testimony.

—Wendell Berry[1]

No one likes a mindfulness preacher, but everyone loves a mindful teacher. Again and again I have heard stories from teachers who have committed to a mindfulness practice and begin having administrators and other teachers ask what they've been doing differently, why they seem so much more relaxed and happy, and why their classes seem to run so much more smoothly. And this is before the teachers have even begun to offer mindfulness-based lessons!

Look at your own life. If you have been committing to your

---

1. Copyright © 2010 by Wendell Berry from *What are People For?* Used by permission of Counterpoint.

practice, you can no doubt see some shifts, internally and externally. With the foundation of your mindfulness practice, the transformation in your teaching has already begun. Compassion, authenticity, humbleness, steadfastness, and joyfulness—all these qualities can be cultivated through the mindfulness practices we explored in the previous section. Many of the most beneficial qualities can arise through a committed mindfulness practice.

In this part we explore how to use the foundation of our own mindfulness to build a classroom environment conducive to mindful teaching.

Qualities of a Mindful Teacher

The following positive teaching qualities arise naturally out of a committed mindfulness practice. It's not that you have to try to act compassionate; with heartfulness practice, compassion is naturally generated. Often these qualities are hampered by our stress and lack of external support. Of course we all experience certain gradations of all these positive qualities throughout our days. Hopefully you will begin experiencing these healthy states arising more and more in moments throughout your day. These passing states of compassion, attention, and authenticity can become enduring traits of your teaching as you continue with a diligent mindfulness practice.

Compassion

Heartfulness practice can cultivate our compassion toward our students and ourselves. The manner in which we offer our knowledge is always relational, and therefore the level of care or coldness in which we offer it will have a great effect on the way the information is received and integrated. Intelligence must be married with kindness for the information we offer to be used for the benefit of the students.

When we see a student being resistant, distracted, or even obstinate, we can use our mindfulness to see the student within the student. Instead of looking at his or her external actions, we can keep our commitment to looking more deeply at the child who is acting out of fear, aggression, or pain. We can ask ourselves what basic needs this student is really trying to meet and clearly see the strategies he or she is using. When we can find our compassion, we can be a much-needed caring figure in this child's life while responding skillfully to his or her complex needs.

Understanding

With a mindfulness practice, we can learn to look more deeply at ourselves and our students. As we practice mindfulness we begin to watch our thoughts and emotional patterns and generally understand ourselves better. As we see ourselves more deeply we can also witness how easy it is to lay our assumptions, judgments, and prejudices onto the world around us.

Often we can put our students into boxes and forget to walk into class each day looking afresh at the people in front of us. We have no idea what is truly happening within the mind, heart, and body of another human being. When we become aware of our assumptions, we open our eyes, which opens our hearts, which can create caring and supportive relationships. When we develop real interest in others, we offer our students the gift of being truly seen. Then the world becomes so much more interesting and beautiful for us as well.

Boundaries

With mindfulness we can gain ever greater awareness of how the world affects us and how we affect the world. By reading our inner stress barometer, we can learn to set boundaries that are aimed at taking care of ourselves. We can start noticing when we have overextended ourselves and need to learn the amazing power of the word *no*. We can develop discernment and notice when students or colleagues are projecting their difficult emotions onto us. Instead of getting caught in the drama sphere, we can respond to their pain with compassion and understanding. With respectful boundaries we learn to take care of our own hearts and to set up a lifestyle that make us healthy, happy, and effective in our teaching.

We need to be mindful when setting boundaries that we are not simply creating a doctrine where everyone needs to do what the teacher says just because that's the way it is. We want to perpetually look deeply at ourselves and the needs of our students to discern the most appropriate boundaries for the student. For trust and safety to develop in a class-room, children need respectful boundaries to be set and modeled by their teacher. Appropriate boundaries do not limit a student, just as a canvas doesn't limit an artist. In fact, boundaries offer students the space in which they can feel secure enough to learn, be creative, and thrive. We sometimes have to act as the external neocortex for kids, modeling emotional regulation when they cannot do it themselves.

Attention

Much is said about the attention deficit disorder epidemic in our youth. One alternative vantage point is that a major cause of ADD is actually a deficit of attention being given *to* our students. We are living in the same age of information distraction that our students are growing up in. To offer quality attention to our students, we need to learn how to slow down ourselves and pay attention to our students' needs without so much stress.

One of the clearest benefits from a committed mindfulness practice is the development of focused attention. We expand the breadth of moments in a day in which we are present to the world around us, rather than being lost in thought. When we are directly present to our students, we are able to track each student's individual needs. Students feel seen and we as teachers can feel greater competency. We can shift out of the frantic need to succeed and turn our classrooms into laboratories of presence, where we are collaboratively cultivating our attention.

Intention

As teachers, we hold clear intentions for our students' healthy development. To do this it's important to think of the difference between intention and expectation. *Intentions* are essential. Our *expectations*, on the other hand, are usually our own projections of what we think our students need. Expectations keep us from staying present to our students' ever-changing selves. When we teach from expectations, we are bound, at some point, to be discouraged and disappointed and miss important opportunities to contribute to the lives of our students. When we teach with good intentions and learn to be flexible with change, we can support our students and the class as a whole from moment to moment.

If you are canoeing down a river, it is crucial to focus on where you are headed. You hold the intention of going in that particular direction. The nature of a river is that it will turn you many directions before you reach your desired spot. We understand that to be part of the experience of canoeing. In the same way a mindful teacher needs to be incredibly flexible with the current of her classroom, while at the same time maintaining focus on her intention to transmit knowledge. Our vision is only as good as our ability to adapt it to the world in which it is emerging. Remember to clarify your intentions for your classroom while checking that your expectations are not getting in the way.

Authenticity

It is important to look at other master teachers and learn their strategies, but at the end of the day the most inspiring teachers are those who are fully being themselves. The message of mindfulness is that you are perfect exactly as you are. We must first embody this before we teach it. With our own self-acceptance we don't have to spend so much time and energy hiding our vulnerability and trying to somehow be better than we already are. Modeling this transparency can be very relieving and inspiring to students.

When teacher are able to admit their own humanity, the students enter a room in which it is safe to be themselves. In mindfulness practice we can admit our own wild minds, our chaotic emotions, and our clumsy bodies. Instead of our usual concealment of embarrassment and stressed striving toward perfection, we can let it all hang out and laugh with each other in the relaxed enjoyment of nonjudgmental community. Instead of picking a scapegoat or forming fractionalized teams, a class can learn to be present with its own imperfections with lightness and care. Humor that does not involve put-downs is a great heart opener. Humor that shows us our common humanity, rather than humor at the expense and isolation of another, lets us all feel safe to be our silly and work-in-progress selves.

Essential Ingredients of a Mindful Classroom

✺

We've created a safe, respectful, honest culture in our classroom that allows for thoughts, feelings, wiggles, frustrations and anything else that might be going on. The atmosphere is that whatever you notice just is and it's okay. After our guided sit, kids always have the opportunity to share about their experience. I'm moved on a daily basis by what they are able to articulate.

—Jennifer Harvey, first grade teacher

Following are some recommendations on how to incorporate mindfulness into your school or youth-based setting to cultivate an environment that is conducive to inner connectedness, emotional health, and social fluency. Remember, though, that systemic change is always more productive than simply offering these practices in one classroom. For the greatest effect, we want the whole school to be practicing together, we want to be training families in compassionate parenting, and we want the communities we send our children into to continue supporting the qualities they are cultivating with mindfulness.

Mindful Mornings

Before the day begins, remember to do your own mindfulness practice. If you can, it's wonderful to find a group within your own work environment to sit with for 10 to 30 minutes each day. You could try doing a heartfulness practice, sending yourself and your students kind wishes. Finding your own attention, balance, and open heart is imperative before entering the swirl of the day.

When students arrive, see if you can greet everyone with direct attention and a sense of care. Endeavor to see each student without putting him or her in a box created by your expectations. As much as possible, remember that the greatest teaching impact comes through relationships—your emotional accessibility and your compassionate presence throughout the day supports the child's ability to learn.

Scheduling Mindful Moments

Scheduling a formal mindful moment in the beginning of the day is conducive to group cohesion and will help everyone feel more safe and attentive. This mindful moment can take many forms. It could simply be a time to practice any of your mindfulness lessons, such as breathing, listening, or movements. It could also be a moment to sit together in silence. This is a wonderful opportunity to pass around a talking piece and have everyone share briefly on a topic. A talking piece can be a stick, a squishy ball, or any other object that one holds when they are speaking and everyone else listens to the holder. If the whole school, students and teachers, can meet together in the beginning of the day to sit silently or have a mindful school meeting, so much the better.

Mindful moments are also helpful when there is a lot of commotion in class, or when an emotional experience has arisen, such as a disagreement or a fight between students. It is very beneficial to let students themselves ask for a mindful class moment before a test or whenever there is a lot of stress.

It can also be very helpful to hold a mindful moment right before school gets out or when students come back from recess. Scheduled around transitions, mindfulness practices can be very helpful in bringing students back to a place of stillness throughout the day.

Peace Corner

Linda Lantieri has pioneered the peace corner concept that is now being used in schools around the world. A peace corner is a safe, nurturing, dedicated space somewhere in a classroom or other room in the school. It is best if the corner is collaboratively created with the students. Examples of what would be in this corner are things like tactile objects to play with, coloring materials, or soothing music on an MP3 player. The corner is decorated with pillows, fabric, and other nourishing objects.

Students are self-referred to the peace corner. This is not a space that a teacher sends the students; youth can go there whenever they want. Students go to the corner when they are feeling dysregulated, and they come back out when they are ready to learn. Most teachers find that students go to the corner right before they would usually act out and they don't stay in for too long. All the teachers I have spoken with said that their students only go to the corner for 5 or 10 minutes and do not use the space to skip out on lessons.

We can create a peace corner, and there's no reason to stop at just a corner. We can make the whole classroom and the whole school peaceful. Take care when choosing the art, lighting, and seating arrangements in your room. Take a seat in the students' chairs and see what the learning environment feels like. What would make your nervous system feel more relaxed and ready to learn? Ask the kids as well. The students may have some wonderful ideas about how to create a more conducive environment, and this opens up a dialogue in which students feel that their well-being is truly being considered.

Using Mindfulness Language

Once students have experienced some mindfulness training, there is some basic language that can be used in your classroom. You will find lessons with this language in the Mindfulness Lessons and Practices section. Through the lessons, students learn the language of their sensation, emotions, and thoughts. Building a mindfulness vocabulary will help students speak articulately about their inner lives so they can communicate better with each other and with you.

Students will learn what it means to put on a mindful body. A mindful body means that we are paying attention to the sensations inside of our bodies and aware of the space around us. It also means that we are aware of our two legs of mindfulness: our focus and our relaxation. It is great when going on a field trip or to recess to invite students to "put their mindful bodies on," so they know to be careful and aware.

Another core concept is the anchor breath. The anchor breath is a focusing exercise in which we notice the way our breathing feels in our bellies. We can tell students that even when there is a lot of chaos in their lives, the anchor breath can bring them back to feeling calm and collected. Once students know about their anchor breath, teachers and even other students can remind them about it whenever a stressful situation arises. A principal may even say over the loudspeaker that since it is testing week, everyone can remember that they have their anchor breath whenever they need it.

Heartfulness is another important word that is helpful to remind students about. Heartfulness designates the mindfulness practices that focus on cultivating emotions like happiness and compassion, while working consciously with emotions, such as anger and sadness when they advise. Once students learn to send kind and caring thoughts, we can bring them back to their heartfulness whenever there is something difficult happening or if someone is feeling really emotional.

Many teachers offer their students lessons on how their brains work. You can describe the reptilian brain, the mammalian brain, and the neocortex. The reptilian brain is the part of the brain that motivates our hungers, desires, protection, and many behaviors that can be very reactionary. Our mammalian brain motivates our emotions and is what rules much of our relational behaviors. The neocortex is the part of brain that creates higher reasoning and can regulate the rest of the brain, like the captain of a ship. You can also describe the amygdala as the part of the brain that is correlated with impulsivity. I have often heard students saying, "My amygdala made me do it." Or they will say, "My lizard brain wanted to grab that ball from Tom but my neocortex stopped me from doing it."

Making Agreements

Whether you are working in a school, a juvenile detention center, or a one-on-one therapy setting, it is invaluable to begin with co-created agreements. To foster a safe space where students will feel comfortable to share and be themselves, we can invite them into a democratic process of agreement making. The practice of group decision making itself is an amazing collaborative learning experience. There is also far less resistance to rules when they have been collectively created.

Of course there are always rules set by the teacher that are not up for debate. Offering explanations for these rules is important. All rules should be in place to create a safe and inspiring setting for the youth, so explaining their purposes should be fairly straightforward. If you have a rule that there will be no harming other students in class, it is simple to explain that you care for the safety of each student and want them agreeing to creating a protected space so everyone can relax, learn, and be happy. If it is hard to explain why the rule is in place, it may not be a very good rule. You can begin making agreements with students by explaining why you have the class rules the way you have them.

To create shared group agreements, you can begin by identifying common values. You can write down all the values that students think make the ideal classroom. Some examples would be safety, respect, fairness, and fun.

The next step would be to get students to go around and share agreements that they believe will cultivate one of the group values. For a value such as respect, for example, students may say "No put-downs" or "No taking other people's stuff."

After all these agreements have been written down, the class can go around and see if they can form a consensus on any of the agreements.

Next you can discuss what the effect would be if these agreements were broken. Have a dialogue of how a particular value, trust, for example, would be affected if the agreement was broken, and what steps the class would need to take to cultivate trust again.

You can write all the agreements on a piece of paper that will go on the wall. If the class decides they want to make a new agreement or change a previous one, they can take the paper down and have a new discussion. Agreements can become an ongoing discussion as the class negotiates new experiences.

This type of discussion empowers students to co-create classroom agreements, which means they will not feel as if they have to fight against the rules. The students will in turn internalize the agreements as they have arisen out of what is important to them.

Creating agreements in any setting is foundational, and you can give them time to be established. This empowers the students while taking some pressure off the teacher. As the group learns to regulate itself, individual students cultivate their own inner regulation.

Mindfulness Is Always Optional

Mindfulness should always be an option for those who want it and optional for those who don't. When mindfulness is mandated, students may miss out on the beauty of what is being offered because they are resistant to being told what to do.

When it is optional, students get to own it for themselves. They get to look at mindfulness with open eyes and decide for themselves if this is something that is beneficial.

Mindfulness classes also should not be limited to those students who have excelled in class or have "earned" the opportunity. Even if a child is being distracting or difficult, make sure not to exclude them from mindfulness time. Sometimes a class needs to go slow to bring everyone on board rather than trying to speed up by getting rid of obstacles. Mindfulness is for everyone; if the interest is there, offer it.

Often students who do not want to participate can sit on the side of the room or be welcomed simply to sit silently in their seat and not follow along. It is very common after a few session for students to become interested just from overhearing what is going on or from hearing what their friends are saying. It is far more productive to let a child sit out in the beginning and enter later of their own interest than to mandate participation from the beginning and have to drag them along the whole time. If mindfulness is being pushed, it is not mindfulness.

Council Practice

Council is a communication structure that invites nonhierarchical dialogue and deep listening. The practice uses the attributes we cultivate with mindfulness by encouraging mindful listening, authenticity, and empathy. Council is appropriate for all age groups. Little children love being able to have turns to be fully heard, and the practice helps them learn how to be patient and listen empathically. Older students can use council as a way to integrate the mindfulness lessons. Council can be used to share the insights they have gained and questions or difficulties that arise.

To create a council, it is imperative to first create a safe space. To do this, the classroom chairs can be brought into a circle, and you can make sure there will be no interruptions. Explaining and getting agreement that everything is confidential is also imperative. You can ring a bell, set a teddy bear in the center of the room, or do some other ritual to signify the beginning of council. Beginning and ending with a ritual helps create containment.

Using a "talking piece" helps create consistency of one person speaking and everyone else listening. You could use a squishy ball or any other object to have students hold when they are speaking. When one person is speaking, they are invited to speak from the heart. Everyone else is welcomed to practice mindful listening to really hear the speaker. The sharing can be popcorn style, where anyone can raise their hand to speak when they want, or sharing can go in a circle. No one is forced to speak in council and can always pass, though you may encourage the quiet ones to speak up.

To prompt conversation, there is a council story, quote, or question. In mindfulness classes, council is an ideal way for students to discuss their experiences. Students can read a story or quote that pertains to the lesson theme and have a discussion of how they see this in their lives. Question about students' social and emotional lives can open up important discussions about how to integrate mindfulness practice into their lives.

Taking Care of the Teachers

As we have seen again and again, teachers need to remember to take care of themselves first. One way we can do this is to offer ourselves the same practices and mindful moments we are offering the students throughout the day. Another way is through weekly mindfulness meetings.

This can simply be a time where teachers get together and sit silently for 30 minutes, then have a discussion. You may want to listen to a guided mindfulness practice, or, following the sitting, a talk on mindfulness that you can then discuss. If it is possible to have 10 minutes in the beginning or end of every day to sit together with all the staff or even a smaller group, this will greatly benefit everyone.

Having regular professional development days where a mindfulness teacher leads a prolonged period of silent practice will help teachers deepen their practice. If teachers are inspired by this, they can seek out external practice centers. There are many retreat centers and community sitting groups that can help individuals further their practice.

Working with Diversity and Inclusion

If you've come here to help me, you're wasting your time. But if you've come because your liberation is bound up with mine, then let us work together.
—Aboriginal activists group, Queensland, 1970s

On the evening after the Sandyhook Elementary School shooting tragedy, I had been scheduled to give an online talk to the 90 participants of the Mindful Education Institute on how to work with destructive emotions. I talked about the importance of schools and communities learning to grieve and heal together. Teachers shared how they were talking to their students about the tragedy and how deeply the murders had effected them. Then Patrick Schirmer, one of the teachers in our program, shared a profound and difficult conversation he had with his class. He had brought up the Sandyhook shootings with his 10th-grade class, which was of predominantly African American heritage. Some of the students felt very sad and disturbed by the killings, whereas others were angry, saying that the shooting was getting too much news when black people are killed every day in their neighborhoods and no one seems to care.

Patrick, as a skilled mindfulness educator, opened the door to this conversation with a real interest in the anger and pain each student was feeling, without judgment. This fueled a deep conversation of the latent anger the students had about the killing of people they had personally known. All the students had their own grief they wanted to share, whether it was about Sandyhook, Oscar Grant (a local shooting of a man by transit police), or a family member of theirs. If Patrick had told the students that they were wrong for not feeling sad about Sandyhook, he would be missing the authentic feelings of the students. Instead, he opened an inquiry into the truth of each student's inner world.

Mindful awareness can lead to understanding, which can lead to compassion, which can lead to empathic action. In one day I sometimes drive from teaching in a school in the flats of Oakland a few miles up into the Berkeley Hills to a privileged private school, where instead of chain-link fences around concrete yards there are redwood trees and open meadows. The 90 percent African American population in the impoverished Oakland school will be flipped to 90 percent white students in the affluent Berkeley Hills school.

The effects of an impoverished upbringing, in comparison to an affluent one, is one of the greatest predictors for school achievement. When we really open our eyes to the disparity in our educational system, we can't help but have our hearts broken. Once we are aware of privilege and discrimination, we can hopefully gain greater understanding of the dynamics in our communities and work toward equity.

Not only do children from wealthy families do far better in school than impoverished students, the rich–poor achievement gap has risen 40 percent in the past 30 years (Reardon, 2013). There is a negative cycle that students are set up for. Impoverished students are far more likely to drop out of school, develop addictions, and end up incarcerated. Once this cycle begins, it's hard to break. Nearly one-quarter of kids in the United States live in poverty. Half of these kids will still be in poverty at age 35, a third will not graduate from high school, and they have an eight-year lower life expectancy (Emanuel, 2012). There are many beautiful stories about the resilience of youth who went down dangerous roads and were able to break out of this negative track, and of course we should always strive to help those in need, but of course, the most conducive way to support youth is to set up conditions in which the cycle doesn't begin in the first place.

Teaching mindfulness to students in impoverished and disenfranchised communities holds great promise. Children who grow up with neglect, domestic violence, and other forms of environmental trauma can particularly benefit from the emotional regulation tools, stress relief, and impulse control techniques offered by mindfulness. Mindfulness can be a home base of stability and an inner lifeline in a tumultuous young life.

If the teachings are presented without adequate cultural understanding or relevance, however, we very well may disempower the students we seek to serve. Let's say we are teaching mindfulness to an incarcerated 16-year-old African American who grew up in foster care and has ended up in the prison system. There is a good chance the authentic and justified emotional experience of this youth will involve a lot of anger and grief. Although impulse control would be very useful for this young man, we would want to be wary that we were not just trying to get him to calm down and suppress his feelings. His anger is justified, and mindfulness can perhaps help him feel the anger, explore it, and find a way to productively channel it.

Most administrators and teachers are not looking at ways to put those in their care in touch with their anger; they would simply like their students to become easier to deal with. In fact some people might prefer that all the diversity issues just go away so that everyone can get along. But oppression, slavery, and class division have been with us since before written record. We must work with privilege, oppression, and diversity in the same way that we practice mindfulness in our minds, bodies, and hearts. Instead of trying to change what we find, we can open the door of presence and understanding.

As always, with mindfulness, we begin with our own practice. We must explore our own biases. Regardless of our racial or cultural background, we certainly have picked up some unconscious biases through our family and culture. Don't worry, we all have them. By using our mindful awareness to witness thought patterns and unconscious beliefs, we can gain greater awareness so that we are not perpetuating discriminatory behaviors. As we get to know children, we may realize that we have judgments and biases toward them. Our awareness is always an opportunity to see through the lines and connect with all students as they truly are. We need to be brave enough to ask ourselves, "How am I perpetuating oppression and racism?"

There are racial, gender, sexual preference, body type, and many other norms that we are expected to fit into. We have to act more masculine or feminine, we have to be cool in specific ways, and of course we have to hide any aspects of ourselves that don't fit in. All the names we were called and the names others were called make a blueprint of what is safe and what is not, what is acceptable and what is not. We have to shrink to fit. We watch mothers who learned they would only be accepted if they were thin then judge their daughters for their weight, repeating the same cruel putdowns, trying to "help." We watch a parent telling a child not to trust people from another race, trying to "protect" them, when really it is the parent's fear that is poisoning another generation. We need to begin with admitting our own fears and biases, for only then can we break the chain of perpetuation.

Once we take our students out of the boxes we have put them in, we can see them as they really are. You can never assume that you know what lies in the inner world of a child. When you are genuinely interested in who your students are, they can feel it. They can sense that someone cares. Some children have never felt really cared for or seen. When we get interested, kids can remember that there is something truly special inside of them and gain the bravery to show the world who they really are. Getting interested in your students means learning about how they see the world, what their family life is like, and what cultural perspectives they carry with them. We learn about the diversity of each child so we can honor their differences, not so that we can make them all the same.

In teaching diverse students, we need to understand cross-cultural perspectives of learning and values. The variety of values among Asian American, African American, Latino, and Native American youth is immense. Values within different Native American tribes or Asian American subgroups are vast as well. It's incredibly important to do some research about the ethnic identity of your students, and the best research you can do is to talk with your students and their families. Family val ues, perspectives on the importance of education, and other worldviews that parents are raising their children with may vary from your own way of seeing the world.

Our mindfulness practice can help us let go of our static worldview and understand the diverse ways of being in the world. Children grow up with very different types of discipline and relationship to authority. To teach we need to understand how each student learns.

As we honor and support diversity, we also need to be conscious of how sensitive this subject is. You can expect to make mistakes again and again and learn to take your foot out of your mouth. For example, some children do not have parents or have parents of the same gender; be conscious when talking about families not to make statements like, "In this gratitude practice let's think of our parents." When speaking and creating lessons, be sensitive to children's relationships to their own gender, sexuality, race, religion, and so on. We can help students become proud of their differences and backgrounds, but we need to do this with great care, sensitivity, and discernment.

Mindful Pointers

- Get interested. Do some research about the populations and cultures you are working with. The best way to do research is simply by being with students and their families. Get to know what is interesting to your students and how they live their lives.
- Cultural and religious traditions have different ways that they view emotions. Some cultures, for example, are less

emotionally expressive, and heartfulness practice may therefore be more vulnerable for these students.

- Be yourself. Don't try to act as if you are a member of the culture you are teaching. You don't need to pick up slang or dress differently. Be authentic and let the students know who you are and what your life is like. Be unapologetically you.
- Offer opportunities to explore ancestry, culture, and family history. Support students in gaining pride and connection to their history. Help students learn about each other and respect each other's diversity.

Working with Stress and Trauma

❈

Jose clenches the red squishy ball in his hand like prey in the jaws of a lion. His eyes, however, are closed, and gradually his shoulders begin to fall and the pace of his breath begins to slow. His fist uncoils little by little with each breath, like the petals of a flower opening, until finally the ball slips from his hand and bounces to the ground, rolling over to Gerardo, who is looking in amazement back at Jose. The rest of us—myself and four 13-year-old boys—are looking at each other with awed smiles. We know that something profound has just taken place.

These boys are entangled in a complex gang culture that permeates their school, their friends, and their families. I am working as a therapist at their school and leading mindfulness-based anger management groups. For months we have been practicing the basics: mindful breathing, heartfulness, and awareness of difficult emotions. Inviting them beneath their tough exteriors and into more vulnerable, emotional realms is an edgy process. Their ire sometimes ends up directed at me, or they taunt each other, and it takes all of my own mindfulness practice to stay grounded, patient, and open-hearted.

These boys—on the very frontier of manhood—love to act cool and tough, though their fear and insecurities are easily seen through the bravado. I see it as my job to honor and support the development of these new men, while simultaneously nurturing the little boys inside. When I offer a mindfulness practice for the first time, they sit silently for a few minutes before making rude noises and kicking each other. Yet after only a few classes they begin to say things like, "This is weird, it actually makes me really calm," or "It's like I am alone and I don't need to worry about anything."

Although youth may initially resist mindfulness practices, once they have experienced the direct beneficial effects in their minds and bodies, the practices become allies that they rely on.

When I feel like the students I am working with have adequate tools for recognizing their emotions and working with them, I start to address the anger more directly. We have a red ball we often use as a talking piece. When someone speaks they hold the ball, and then shoot it into the little basketball hoop to conclude their turn. They enjoy this, so I take the red ball and tell them we're going to play a game called Anger Ball. "Who has something they're feeling upset about right now?" I ask. Jose pops his hand up immediately. I toss him the ball, and he launches into a tirade about some kid from another school who is bad-mouthing his Dad. Jose's dad has just been taken to prison for molesting his sister. Obviously kids making fun of his father is hitting a deeply raw nerve. One can only imagine how confusing and painful these emotions are.

"If I see that kid I'll rip him apart!" He furiously squeezes and twists the ball, spewing his words in a steady, unbroken stream of anger and anguish.

"Do you see what you're doing with that ball?" I ask him.

"Yeah! This is what I want to do to him!"

"Okay, go for it. We're all with you. Supporting you. You can be as angry as you need to be." He looks at me for a moment, wondering if I am for real. His eyes flare and he throws the ball down, stomps on it, and throws it against the wall. By now he is panting, and the room feels like a shaken soda can ready to pop. I offer him a seat and gently ask the group to assist by sending him some heartfulness while he focuses all his energy into the ball with his hands.

"Jose, you have as long as you need; just hold the ball with all of your feelings, and at the same time practice your vacuum breath (Roots of Emotion Lesson, p. 217), and see if you can let it suck up the anger. When the anger goes, you can drop the ball. Until then we will just sit here with you and do our own vacuum breaths to support you."

I watch him claw at the ball for about three or four more minutes, and then slowly—as he breathes and the rest of the boys breathe with him—his whole body relaxes. The tension in the room eases palpably, and slowly, his hand uncoils and the ball falls to the ground. All the boys sit there for a moment with wide-open eyes. "Let me try that," says Gerardo.

The next week in group, Gerardo tells us the story of how he got jumped by two kids who were trying to start a fight. "I felt my fists tighten, and then I remembered the anger ball and started breathing. I relaxed and looked up at them; they seemed kind of confused and scared themselves. I just told them to calm down and I walked away. They cursed at me a bit but it didn't stick." By stepping out of the usual pattern of emotional reactivity, Gerardo was able to observe, objectively and respond with discernment.

Many other stories can be told in this vein, with youth beginning to change habitual destructive patterns.

Jose divines, "I guess the anger ball is like that hot potato game where people are passing it around because it's too hot.

One person steps to another with their anger, and that person hits someone else, and we keep passing it around because no one knows mindfulness."

Research on trauma, neglect, and abuse have given us a window into their tragic effects on the brain, on gene expression, and into the patterns that those suffering from them develop over a lifetime. The Adverse Childhood Experience (ACE) study has shown how difficult early childhood experiences set a path for obesity, drug use, criminality, and other destructive behaviors. "The ACE Study also showed that as the ACE score increased the number of risk factors for the leading causes of death increased. Thus, persons with high ACE scores are later at much higher risk for health and medical conditions resulting from their choice of remedies for their pain. While these approaches are effective in the short term, they often have dire long-term consequences such as serious chronic health and social problems" (Felitti et al., 1998).

Kids need to know what to do with toxic stress. If they are not given adequate practices and venues to relieve their tensions, the basic physics of the body necessitates some other form of release. If they can't do so in a healthy way, kids can choose the endless unhealthy opportunities at their disposal. Instead of trying to stop drug use, promiscuity, violence, and other destructive behaviors, we need to offer healthy alternatives. With love, care, and attention, even children in the most terrible environments can grow up resilient and healthy.

Every child grows up with some stress, but many grow up with significant trauma, whether it stems from neglect, a random accident, or ongoing abuse. Trauma distances us from the present moment, disassociates us from our bodies, and turns us away from our emotions and difficult sensations. Mindfulness, on the other hand, returns us to the present moment, bringing our attention back to our emotions, sensations, and our ever-transforming experience.

Trauma arises when a distressing experience or an ongoing difficulty is so great that we lose our capacity to respond adequately. Stephan Cope puts it well in his introduction to the book *Overcoming Trauma through Yoga* when he says, "In Trauma, the body's alarm systems turn on and then never quite turn off. And we experience the intense suffering of never truly feeling relaxed, at ease in life, always intensely on guard, with the primitive brain constantly scanning for threat or opportunity. Our inner sentry is always on watch" (Emerson, 2011).

With trauma, our inner sentry is always on high alert as if the initial trauma was still physically imminent, even if the current situation is completely safe. If a child is having a trauma reenactment, which means that they are reliving a traumatic experience, the usual therapeutic interventions resemble embodied mindfulness practices. One must invite the student to orient themselves back into the room, helping them feel their body in their chair, seeing the colors and shapes around them, hearing the sounds of their immediate surroundings. You want to help the student reorient to the present moment, where they are safe and sound.

Trauma separates us from the present moment, so mindfulness is a good antidote to invite kids into a restful space in their bodies. It is also imperative to help kids find a place where they feel safe. Some trauma trainings work on helping people find a safe space they can return to in their minds whenever they get too afraid. With mindfulness we are cultivating an inner experience of stillness, safety, and happiness. Creating this base of safety gives kids with a history of trauma, or continue to live in traumatic situations, a refuge.

The hope is that mindfulness can intervene to relax the "inner sentry" and bring the nervous system back to its balanced state. With the integrative effects that mindfulness has on the brain, the hope would be that the inevitable stressors of life will not get caught in the body in the first place. It has been shown how two people can share the same threatening experience but respond to it very differently—one with trauma and the other with only a harrowing story. The determining factor seems to be whether the person has the inner skills to meet the experience with resilience and hope rather than hopelessness and shame. In *Waking the Tiger*, Peter Levine says, "Traumatic symptoms stem from the frozen residue of energy that has not been resolved and discharged. This residue remains trapped in the nervous system where it can wreak havoc on our bodies and spirits" (Levine, 1997).

Most of us are familiar with the idea of the fight-or-flight response. The third option that is less often spoken of but just as real is the freeze response. If a mouse sees a hawk flying close, for example, its whole body may freeze. If the hawk flies away, the mouse will go through an elaborate shaking response. Humans have this same freeze instinct, but most of us don't remember how to shake out the stress. This leaves many of us storing unshaken stress in our bodies.

Long ago we knew how to naturally release our trauma and stress, but now, as the boys in my anger management class understood so well, we pass the hot potato around. When we don't teach our children the inner resources to meet difficult experiences or give them appropriate methods to release trauma, they carry it into their bodies and inflict this pain on either themselves or the world around them.

The ideal situation is for students to have a safe and corrective experience of being able to release their stress so they can come back to rest. We can offer students the requisite experience of a safe interpersonal space to rewire their relationship to past stressors. The nervous system cannot learn a new way forward until it has had a true visceral experience of another way. The brain literally needs to be rewired, and this rewiring can only happen with repeated empathic interactions. A student may be extremely mistrusting and resistant to a genuinely caring teacher's mentorship because of a traumatic history of abuse from older people in his or her life. Through the teacher's patience, caring, and understanding, the student may be able to learn that not all older people are unsafe, and some may truly want to help them.

Bessel A. van der Kolk says, "The goal of treatment of PTSD (post-traumatic stress disorder) is to help people live in the present, without feeling or behaving according to irrelevant demands to the past" (van der Kolk, 1994). Mindfulness is the doorway to the present moment. We systematically teach students how to witness the hijacking system of trauma and invite them back into their bodies in the present moment.

Embodied mindfulness can integrate a stressed system, but we need to be very aware that mindfulness practices can also provoke difficult emotional responses in children that can have adverse affects if there is not adequate containment. Usually kids learn to build emotional armoring, and when a mindfulness class opens a safe and caring atmosphere these locked-in emotions may spring forth. We want students to have a safe space to bring their full emotional experience, but if the container is not adequately held, the release will be a retraumatization rather than a corrective experience.

There is profound healing possible through mindfulness, but we need to be very aware of the mechanism of trauma and the effects of different mindfulness practices. In David Treleaven's thesis on meditation and trauma (Treleaven, 2013), he raises a crucial inquiry into the dangers of mindfulness becoming a dissociative practice rather than an embodying and healing one. Treleaven explores the most scientifically relevant and effective trauma trainings such as Peter Levine's somatic experiencing as well as sensorimotor psychotherapy. Though he concurs with all of the research on the health benefits of mindfulness, he argues that without adequate understanding of trauma a mindfulness teacher could unwittingly push a student into a sensory awareness that was overly distressing. Treleaven says, "According to Levine, attending to somatic contractions with great intensity is not recommended, especially for individuals with a history of trauma. While this is not to suggest that traumatized individuals should not meditate or dance, it asks teachers within these traditions to become knowledgeable about the potential pitfalls of contemplative and somatically based practices."

Trauma arises because of a level of somatic distress that the psyche of the individual cannot contain, one that causes them to split off from themselves to protect their basic sanity. We would never throw a child back into an abusive situation in which he or she had been traumatized, but entering back into the somatic experience, without proper therapeutic containment, is ostensibly the same thing as the original trauma. The body is flooded with the same terror, and the protective mechanisms come right back up, reinforcing the old pattern. Treleaven says, "This places traumatized meditators in the precarious position of being mindful of sensations that may perpetuate a fear-immobility spiral."

To mitigate these dangers we need to get thorough training in trauma and stress-related disorders. Not only can we be trained to be sensitive and skilled with our students, we can learn how to care for our own stress and trauma. We all have vicarious stress and trauma from teaching, as well as the scrapes and bruises we collected on our journeys to adulthood. In expanding the capacity to care for ourselves, our hearts stretch open and gain the emotional navigation skills to support students in the landscape of their own hearts.

Mindful Pointers

- It is important to remember that mindfulness practices, particularly heartfulness, can stimulate difficult emotional responses in children. Develop a strong network of collateral resources, such as school therapists, social workers, and local agencies. You can use these resources to consult with and refer students to if they reveal trauma or abuse.

- If you have abuse or trauma in your own history, it can be very healing to seek therapy or trauma support, such as eye movement desensitization and reprocessing, somatic experiencing, or Hakomi. Not only can this help you in transforming your own trauma, it can help you in understanding how to be of support to your students.

- It is extremely important to understand the stressors and traumas of the students you work with. Learn about your students' communities, families, and local environments to gain a greater understanding of their stressors, as well as their resources.

Working with Different Age Groups

Gazing around the room, I watch the students rubbing black and white chess pieces on their faces, clanking them together, and tossing them under desks. These are not preschoolers but high-school honors students who have been admitted to a summer college program to study with teachers such as myself who have them giggling and pretending they are infants. I am teaching experientially, as I always try to do, about Jean Piaget's stages of development. As their well-paying parents imagine their children listening to carefully crafted developmental psychology lectures, I have them regressing into their infant selves.

I explain to the students, "Imagine you are a one-year-old with a chess board in front of you. You are not going to understand the rules of the game and will probably not even care about the kid on the other side of the board. You are interested in the direct physical experience of the chess pieces on your skin, the sounds they make, and the colors you see. You are in Piaget's 'sensorimotor stage.'"

The brain is divided into three parts; the reptilian, mammalian, and neocortex. We can look at the bottom stem of the brain as the foundational element that is built on but never replaced. This area is the root experience of instinct and raw somatic navigation, it is the primary brain region that the sensorimotor stage infant navigates from.

On this part the mammalian brain gets built, with all its emotional and relational experience. As the mammalian brain is developed more, the child enters what Piaget called the preoperational phase, where they gain an experience of the past and the future, which entails abstraction. I tell the high school students, "Now imagine you are five years old and playing chess. You are aware of the person on the other side of the board and that there is a game that you are playing. You are not very good yet at understanding what is happening within the other person. You can play, but you're probably going to want to make up your own rules." The students have fun stacking their pieces together and trying to parallel play until one precocious student begins a play tantrum.

From here the neocortex grows like the cherry on top of the sundae. In Piaget's theory we next arrive at the concrete operational stage. I tell the students, "Imagine you are 10 years old playing a game of chess with a friend. You can understand the rules of the game but can't plan beyond the move in front of you." The students play and I see how the only importance for them is what is right in front of them. They make a move and then fiddle with a piece or play with their hair. They understand rules and games but are not able to stay present to see the moves in advance.

Then I invite the students to be exactly, naturally who they are at 17 years old. They play chess for a few minutes in the formal operational stage, able to think of moves a few turns in advance and relate with the opponent with an emotional understanding of how the game is affecting them. The students get to experientially walk the ladder of millions of years of evolution within a half an hour. They get to watch 17 years of cognitive development in one class.

In all developmental models each stage of consciousness is built on the last, not replacing but adding levels to the foundation. Depending on whether the basic needs of the students are met, the child either evolves naturally to the next stage or has an arrested development. The developmental psychologist Erik Erikson saw two distinct paths of human development. If the child's early life is marked with comfort, dependability, and nourishment, she will gain an inner sense of trust and will look to the world with enthusiasm and optimism. If the conditions are not safe and nurturing, the child will be imprinted with a sense of mistrust and the world will become a dangerous and undependable place. In Erikson's eight life stages model, individuals continue to take these roads of health or disease. Primarily because of our level of support and nurturing, we are lead down the roads of autonomy or shame, initiative or guilt, intimacy or isolation. We know which road we want to be on, which road we want our children to be on, and which way we want our whole world to be headed.

Creating a mindful environment and implementing stage-specific lessons can support students in heading down the roads of initiative, autonomy, and trust. Regardless of what age we are teaching, the essences of the mindfulness lessons stay the same. Even very young children can learn how to witness their own sensations, emotions, and even thoughts. Becoming aware of the mind, heart, and body is possible for all ages, but of course there are different developmental stages to be aware of and different language to be used according to the student's age. By looking at developmental psychology and neuroscience, we can see which teachings are possible and appropriate.

Each lesson in the lesson toolbox includes a note on teaching to K–5th-grade students and 6th–12th-grade students. Within both age groups there is a great range of developmental stages. The stages are broken down to provide you with a better idea of what is generally appropriate for grades K–2, 3–5, 6–8, and 9–12. Of course, each child develops in their own way. I hope these reflections from my own experience teaching mindfulness to youth of all age groups will be helpful to you. Teachers need to pay attention to the developmental stages of their individual class and individual students.

Mindfulness Practices for Grades K–2

Little children live in the present moment far more than most adults do, and we need to remember how many mindfulness lessons we can learn from them every day. Although children are adept at riding the waves of the present moment, they don't know how to ride with nonreactivity. Mindfulness can help them with self-regulation skills as well as developing the empathic ability of understanding what happens inside of others' minds.

Children in this age group are still close to the unfiltered baby awareness that arises without any shame, emotional constriction, or self-limiting beliefs. They are naturally eager, curious, and open to learning and playing. More so than in any other stage, they are open to new practices and ways of seeing the world; in fact, their highly adaptive brains are actively seeking new and varied experiences. Because their minds are so plastic, it is that much more important that we create a loving, nonjudgmental, safe space in which they can learn. Children at this age are developing the habits, beliefs, and relational patterns they will carry into the rest of their lives.

Mindful Implementation

At this age a mindfulness class can last from 10 to 30 minutes. Usually a concept is presented and then there is a short practice. Silent practice, such as mindful breathing, can rarely be held for longer than five minutes. After the practice it's good to have time for sharing and other explorations. Get mindfulness journals for students and use the drawing prompts to help take time to reflect. Students at this age learn best through highly embodied practices such as mindful movements, mindful eating, and the heartful hug. Using props, like putting a teddy bear on a student's belly as they breathe or using a snow globe to bring awareness to their busy minds, are very helpful.

Ritual and routine are ideal ways to integrate these mindfulness practices for five- to seven-year-olds. Having a few minutes of mindful breathing followed by a check-in is a wonderful way to begin and end a school day. Ringing a mindful bell or doing some mindful movements is a great way to play with transitions and work with the class when it is getting rowdy. Finally, remember at this age to say that you are "playing mindfulness." Make it fun!

Mindful Pointers

- Create a warm, safe space in which students can learn. When you create a place for them to be themselves, they'll feel safe enough to share their emotions and their true inner experience. Make your classroom a place students enjoy being.
- Children already have the capacity to be aware of their own sensations, emotions, and thoughts at this age. Learning the language of the body, heart, and mind in an expe-

riential way builds the foundation for greater cognitive understanding down the line.

- Students may not conceptually understand why they are doing the exercises, but they don't need to intellectually comprehend the concept to get the benefit of it. Students will somatically recognize the importance of these practices and even do them on their own when the practice has been reinforced often enough experientially.

- Children at this age have a pronounced need to feel appreciated and seen. There is a strong tendency to look to teachers for approval. The ethics we embody are the greatest factors of what students at this age will learn.

- We need to remember to keep within the range of our students. When a student feels left behind, it can create shame and self-criticism. To foster an inner sense of strength and success, stay attuned to where each student is.

- Create clear structures for students to learn within. Like a sandbox, children need to feel clear boundaries to play and thrive. Make sure to hold strong and compassionate boundaries, within which the students can be completely free.

- Students at this age are still coming to understand cause and effect. This is a great time for them to begin learning how emotions look on other faces and to play games that cultivate empathy and understanding.

Mindfulness Practices for Grades 3–5

Children at this age are still in a natural state of wonder and creativity. Pablo Picasso famously said, "Every child is an artist. The problem is staying an artist when you grow up." While children at this age retain a great sense of imagination and enthusiasm, their rational minds are rapidly developing. When they report emotions and awareness of inner experiences, their statements are much more reliable than those of younger children. Mindfulness practices for third-, fourth-, and fifth-graders are aimed at broadening self-awareness while helping them maintain the creative wonder of their young minds.

With the evolution of self-awareness can come self-criticism and insecurity. There is a great need to please at this stage, and relationships are extremely important. Social anxiety and performance anxiety can arise at this time in a child's life. Impulse control, calming strategies, and other self-regulation skills are invaluable mindfulness practices for this age group. Students at this age need a lot of positive reflection. Remember to offer positive feedback without too much praise or blame. Simply offering kind, supportive attention is all that is needed.

Mindful Implementation

Mindfulness lessons can last from 10 to 45 minutes for third- to fifth-graders. Students in this age group are able to spend longer in silent practices, sometimes up to 10 minutes. Along with basic practices, at this grade/age you can begin to incorporate a council dialogue or another type of reflection time. Students can use mindfulness journals for both drawing and writing. Mindful movement games, listening to sounds, and other highly embodied mindfulness explorations are still important bedrocks of practice for this age. Though they are much more able to maintain attention at this age, they are still best engaged through play.

Routine is still very important for students at this age. Aim to have short practices every day at set times. Students can also be empowered to be leading their own practices. Each day of the week, for instance, a different student can get to open class with a mindfulness lesson. Students and teachers can also spontaneously use practices for conflict management, test stress, and other moments of difficulty.

Mindful Pointers

- This grade range is when standardized testing begins in some schools, and many other outside stresses start to effect kids. With mindfulness students can learn to work with their thoughts and stressors in a whole new way.
- Students at this age learn best in a step-by-step fashion. Break lessons into pieces and take plenty of time. Don't move on to the next lesson until everyone is on board.
- Follow the flow of the class. Students at this age have waves of energy that have them buzzing around the room at one moment and crashing with exhaustion the next. Plan lessons around the times of day that are most likely to be the most conducive to quite reflection and be willing to change midstream.
- Students at this age begin to appreciate learning *with* the teacher rather than simply being taught. Students enjoy knowing that you do not know everything and that their views are respected.
- Children begin to appreciate knowing the rational reason for mindfulness lessons. Talk about benefits of the lessons and tie them to things the kids like doing: basketball, jump rope, being better friends. Students at this age can

even begin to learn about neuroscience and how the practices are affecting their brains.

Mindfulness Practices for Grades 6–8

For this age group, mindfulness practices are ideally used to defuse stressors, support inner guidance, and develop impulse control. Adolescents exist in a turbulent world of inner and outer transformation. Their bodies, minds, and social positions are changing drastically. They begin observing the world and themselves closely, wondering who they are and how they fit in. This can be provoke great insecurity and anxiety.

These adolescents are developing their sense of agency, and they yearn to be empowered in their social world and other activities. Adolescents often self-identify as nonchildren, but they are not exactly sure where they fit in society. One ostensible result of this is that peer-to-peer relationships become the most important relationships for kids of this age.

Adolescence is a dangerous time. Students will begin exploring very adult experiences and withdrawing from positive adult role modeling. In some ways they are still very much children, as their impulse control and reasoning are not fully developed, but they often push away from parents and other positive influences. It is vital to honor the independence of students in this age group while maintaining the support and boundaries that adolescents still very much need. Fostering open channels of connection for students helps maintain their trust in looking to adults for guidance as they develop.

Mindful Implementation

For sixth- to eighth-grade students, mindfulness lessons can last from 30 minutes to an hour. Silent practice can last up to 20 minutes if the students are really settling into it. Lessons are taught with explanations of their benefits and how they can be integrated into their lives. Council practices, dyad discussions, and other communication exercises can be used to help students learn how to integrate these practices into their worlds.

Middle-school students often do not stay with an individual teacher but pass from class to class. This necessitates that either the entire school signs up for mindfulness or a teacher simply brings the practices to the students who come in to their classroom. If the latter is the case you will need to find ways to slip in practices here and there. Quick, five-minute lessons can be taught at the beginning of each class, or you can work in moments of breathing and relaxation throughout the class period. To really learn the basics of mindfulness, though, students will need at least a few 20-minute sessions to begin to understand the principles. After-school mindfulness clubs and assemblies can become important ways to meet the needs of this group.

Mindful Pointers

- There can be a great sense of possibility and hope within adolescents, and a teacher's reflections of possibility and hope can support those students in following their dreams.
- Self-doubt and insecurity may rear their heads at this

age. Students are actively looking for who they are and can be filled with comparison and feelings of "not good enough." Mindfulness practices support students, witnessing these thought patterns without feeding them.

- This is the beginning of the age of cool. Heartfulness practices can be seen as very uncool. It is imperative that teachers not be drawn into the culture of cool. Staying with our own self-love and self-assuredness allows us to embody authenticity for students.

- Body changes and gender identity issues are very strong at this age. Bringing self-acceptance and relaxation to the body can be of great support. Learning to be present with their emotional intensity can be a daunting task for adolescents, but they will find that learning to open the heart to whatever is happening in the body is of profound benefit.

- Bullying steps up a notch at this age. Social-emotional skills and communication exercises can help classes, schools, and whole societies address this concern. Understanding the emotions of self and others is much more possible at this point of cognitive development, and cultivating that understanding can be a very effective way of relieving the pressures of bullying, if not ending it all together.

Mindfulness Practices for Grades 9–12

Teenagers have families, friends, teachers, media, and a host of other influences pulling them in many different directions.

They are looking to recognize their own individual identity, having grown out of childhood; they are now constructing their own path. Underneath all the coolness and insecurity there is the deep question of "Who am I?" Teenagers want to fit in, but they also want to be authentic. They want to know what to do to be liked, while simultaneously wanting to be themselves and not having to fake it.

Mindfulness offers teenagers a way to connect to a deeper authenticity and inner compass. It also offers them a more skillful way of interacting with others. Cognitively, mindfulness can help them gain a greater understanding of cause and effect, witnessing how their behaviors affect others and how they want to be treated. Exploring how their minds, hearts, and bodies are affected by the world helps them understand how their actions and thoughts affect others.

At this age students are cognitively equipped to become aware of the needs and wants of the world around them as distinct from their own needs and wants. The result is that teens are particularly capable of learning to listen and talk in ways that resolve conflicts.

The teen years are fraught with the adventures and dangers of risky behaviors. Teens learn to become themselves by pushing limits and breaking patterns. They also run the risk of getting caught in addictive behaviors that can limit their development. Teens are likely to seek an initiatory coming-of-age experience, and if this is not given to them from the outside they will create it for themselves, often in dangerous, self-destructive ways. Creating a supportive transformational environment to safely explore internal and external edges nurtures the healthy development of the adult that the teen is becoming.

Mindful Implementation

For 14–18-year-old students, lessons can last from 30 minutes to an hour and a half. Usually a mindfulness class will start with a new concept, have a practice of 10 to 20 minutes, and then have an extended dialogue or reflection time. Students at this age can really begin gaining an understanding of how the world affects them and how they in turn affect the world.

Since most high school students migrate from classroom to classroom, teachers will need to find a way to introduce moments of practice into classes. At this age, a good option is to have extracurricular mindfulness clubs where the students really have time to communicate among themselves and explore the practices. There are even week-long mindfulness retreats led for teenagers where they practice for full hour-long silent sittings. Even in short practices though, mindfulness lessons can be very supportive for students experiencing the stress of the teen years. Practices can be used before tests, in conflict management, and in other difficult situations. Mindfulness journals can become a reflection exercise that supports inner exploration.

Mindful Pointers

- At this age it is important to support self-determination. Teenagers need to experience mindfulness practice as their own project or it will be yet another thing they feel is forced on them.
- Students can be inspired by the idea of gaining mastery of these practices so that they can succeed in sports, so-

cial relations, and other situations that are exciting for them.

- Life for teens is very peer-centered. It can be important to weave in social components to the training to make it more engaging. You can show students how these practices support self-esteem and strengthen social skills.
- Share with students how kindness is sometimes seen as uncool by teenagers, but that deep down everyone wants to be liked and have friends. You can help students see how cool being kind and compassionate is.
- Be aware of how sensitive teenagers are about body issues (and just about everything.) Teens are far more insecure than any other age group. Mindfulness practices are amazingly supportive in helping teens maintain a grounded sense of self.
- Teens are often very judgmental, and they pick up inauthenticity quickly. When teaching this age group, it is important not to try to impress. Your own authenticity and security will be what is most respected in the long run.
- Giving projects and ways for students to explore these practices themselves will help them make the practices their own. You can empower students to become leaders and to create projects in the community.

PART IV

❋

Mindful Education Curriculum

This curriculum is an offering to you, and if it inspires you and you choose to use it, please continue to develop your own mindfulness practice as the underlying attitude from which you teach. As you would be sure to become a good swimmer before you become a swimming instructor, be sure to learn to swim in the ocean of awareness before inviting your students into these waters.

In this final section we learn practical ways to implement mindfulness into classrooms and other youth-based settings. We will look at how to introduce mindfulness to students in a way that is accessible and with the greatest impact. Then we look at a basic lesson layout in which mindfulness lessons can be best presented, practiced, and integrated.

In this section we will learn how to teach our students the same four categories of mindfulness practices that we learned for ourselves in Part II. These practices correspond to gaining greater awareness of the body, mind, heart, and world. Each lesson comes with learning objectives, sample scripts, age appropriateness, and other important frameworks for the implementation of practices.

There are as many ways to teach mindfulness as there are teachers. The framework set out here is a synthesis of best practices and ways of structuring lessons from my own work in schools from diverse cultures, ages, and locations. These lessons are not a static protocol but more of a palette of colors that you can use to make your own beautiful lessons and classroom environments.

Introducing Mindfulness to Students

❁

By now you are establishing your own mindfulness practice and learning to embody the qualities of a mindful teacher. Now you can explore teaching these mindfulness lessons to your students. Mindfulness is a very different subject than reading, writing, and arithmetic. Academic subjects are like different movies streamed out of a projector. Mindfulness is the process of examining the projector itself. Academic subjects use different parts of the mind, whereas mindfulness goes right to the source and studies the mind directly.

To teach mindfulness it is important to treat the material differently than you would a usual lesson. As much as possible we don't want mindfulness to turn into another subject that students need to be stressed about getting good grades. You can tell the class that they all get an A+ just for having been born. Remember to give yourself an A+ as well; once you've get that sorted out, it's time to jump in.

In this section we explore strategies for cultivating the right conditions in which students can learn mindfulness. You are not giving students any information here; you are inviting them to make their own discoveries. We cannot push mindfulness in the same way that most subjects are taught, or we risk turning it into indoctrination. Mindfulness is an invitation to authenticity, not a behavioral modification.

Remember that you are going to make mistakes at this. The question is not if you will make mistakes, but how much you will learn from them and how kind you can be to your inevitable humanity. Your authenticity and willingness to learn as much, or more, than your students is the greatest mindfulness teaching you can give.

Setting Up the Room

Begin by setting up the room. It's imperative to let the students know that they are being introduced to a new way of seeing the world, interacting with each other, and knowing themselves. To do this it is important to shift the seating arrangement so that everyone is in a circle or some configuration that is more conducive to a sense of equality and openness. You want the space to feel safe, and therefore you will not want an area where people from outside the class can see or hear. Experiment with ways of making the space feel more safe and supportive. You can change the lighting, get comfortable cushions, or take recommendations from the students regarding what would help them to connect to their mindfulness time.

If it is impossible to get the students in a circle, then ask them to turn their chairs toward you. If it is possible within the setting, make the mindfulness classes optional. If students don't want to take part in the class, you can let them sit on the side without distracting anyone. Mindfulness should never feel like a punishment or something that is being pushed. If students want to be part of the group but are being rambunctious, it can be helpful to have a teacher sit next to them, giving them a tactile object to play with, or asking them what they need so as not to be distracting to others.

Introducing Mindfulness

Once the room has been set, you can introduce mindfulness. Before launching into your own definition, ask the group if they have ever heard of mindfulness and, if so, what they have heard. You may get some rather profound responses. If we start with our own definition of mindfulness, later on the youth may just parrot back to us what they think we want them to say, like "when I did mindfulness I felt calm and relaxed." Although this is a very nice statement, if you began by telling them that mindfulness was all about being calm and relaxed, then you have no idea if that was actually their truth.

Inviting Stillness

Just like learning to swim, you cannot learn by standing at the edge of the water; you have to dive in. With this in mind, we next invite students into an experience of mindfulness without any instructions about breath or closing our eyes. Simply ask them to be still and notice. You can say something like, "To learn what mindfulness is we can simply begin by noticing what happens when we get really still. Let every part of your body come into total stillness and see what you notice when we are all so still."

After the class has sat for a few moments, you can ask them what it was like. Remember that there are no wrong answers; we actually want the youth to get to know themselves and then share with us whatever is going on. If they are angry, the perfect mindfulness answer will be "I am angry." If they are relaxed, the perfect answer is "I am relaxed." The true answer is the right answer.

If a student says, "When I was sitting I felt really bored and annoyed," this is great information that you can inquire more deeply into. You may say, "Isn't that interesting that when we slow down for just 30 seconds and look inside, we have so many feelings come up? Why do you think that happens?" Usually one of the things that students say is, "It got really quiet when we got so still." From this, we can invite the youth to remember to be totally quiet when they are sitting so that they are not distracting anyone else.

"Let's sit totally still again, but this time let's notice what it is like to remember to be totally quiet and let our eyes close. If it doesn't feel comfortable to close your eyes, just look down in front of you and don't let your eyes get distracted. Notice what you experience when you are just sitting still and quiet without looking at anything."

When we invite youth to close their eyes, we need to remember that for some of them this may not feel safe. We are inviting them to withdraw their attention from the visual world and this can feel threatening to some children. You can simply ask these students to focus their gaze on the floor or desk in front of them. Once they practice this, you can again ask them what they noticed. Together as a group you can begin to collaborate on an understanding of what mindfulness is without needing to force ideas on them.

Benefits of Mindfulness

Once students have had their own taste of mindfulness through this initial guided experience, you can offer them a basic description of the core competencies and practices and their benefits. Tell the class how often you will be doing the practices and what they will probably look like. Depending on the age and population of your class, you might consider talking about professional sports teams that practice mindfulness, dancers using their breath to balance, the neuroscience of how mindfulness actually changes the brain, or how it will help students with their reactivity so they won't get into trouble. There are so many benefits to mindfulness that it's easy to find metaphors and stories that can help students understand how this practice can serve them.

Here's an example of something you might say when explaining the benefits of mindfulness: "When we are mindful it is like we are waking up from a dream. All of a sudden when we listen with our mindful ears, we hear little sounds like the lights above us buzzing and the sound of our friend's breathing next to us. All these sounds have been going on all the time, but we were so caught up in our thoughts that we didn't notice. There are so many amazing songs to hear, beautiful passing birds to see, and delicious foods to taste. When we open our mindful awareness, we can play basketball or jump rope with the focus and agility of an Olympic athlete. We can learn to study for a test or play a musical instrument without all the usual distraction, and get things done quickly and easy. Neuroscience shows that mindfulness actually rewires our brains so that we are less reactive so that we won't get into trouble as much. Science is also showing that mindfulness just plain makes us more happy, and what's more important that?"

The Layout of a Mindfulness Lesson

Mindfulness lessons can be integrated into everyday class structures, but when introducing new lessons, it is helpful to give an extended period of time to explore each practice. It is good to give yourself about 15 minutes to introduce a new lesson to elementary-age students. For middle school and high school students, it can be helpful to do a whole hour.

For whatever group you are working with, you want the time to be able introduce the new lesson, do the practice, and have some reflection and integration time. The basic flow set out below works well for students of all age groups.

- Opening Mindful Moment
- Check-In and Report Back
- New Lesson Introduction
- Practice
- Sharing/Council
- Journaling
- World Discovery
- Closing Mindful Moment

Opening Mindful Moment

At the beginning of every mindfulness class, you can start with a mindful moment. If the students have learned a few practices already, you can start with the last lesson you taught. You can simply set it up that you when you ring the bell it is understood that the mindfulness class has begun and everyone practices for a few minutes. Some of the go-to opening lessons are mindful listening, the anchor breath, and mindful movements. Once students have been practicing mindfulness for some time, you can have a student choose and lead an opening practice.

Check-In and Report Back

Once the students have experienced some mindfulness lessons, you can ask them about how they have been using their practice in everyday life. At the end of every class you can offer home study assignments in which they are invited to notice their emotions, their attention, or other theme-specific lessons. This check-in time helps students begin to understand how they are using their mindfulness skills in their everyday lives. As they report back on their findings, the whole class can learn from itself and the students can witness their own growth in a very satisfying way.

New Lesson Introduction

After the check-in you can introduce the next lesson. This is where you would talk about heartfulness, attention, and so on.

It is important to remember not to tell the students what the experience will be like, but simply set up the lesson as an exploration. If you were presenting heartfulness, for instance, you would talk about how you will be teaching them to gain a greater understanding of their emotional world, then you would offer them instructions on how to practice doing that.

Practice

After describing the next lesson, it's time dive into the experiential practice. The many mindfulness curricula build on each other. Generally it is most effective to begin with simple embodiment and attention practices. From these basic lessons you can move deeper into explorations of becoming aware of difficult emotions and being mindful in the world.

Sharing/Council

It's always helpful to give students some time to share how the experience unfolded for them. Listen openly without judgment, and you will learn a lot about your students. Remind the students to share their direct experience without getting lost in stories or ideas about what happened. You can use a council, mindful small group discussion, or other forms of mindful communication.

If you have time, it's great to share a story, quote, or exercise that pertains to the topic of the day. For example, if the lesson involved working with difficult emotions, you may share the quote, "You can't stop the waves, but you can learn how to surf." Then you could use a council practice to go around the room and hear what students thought of this quote. Another option would be to break students into smaller groups to do a project or tell each other their experiences.

Journaling

It's often very helpful to give the students time to reflect in their journals about the lesson. Younger students can draw pictures and older students can write some reflections. If you were doing a gratitude lesson, for example, you might have them draw a picture or write about the things they are grateful for in their lives. These practices help students integrate

and make meaning of whatever lesson they have just experienced.

World Discovery

At the end of every lesson, we can suggest a way to explore the theme at hand in daily life. For example, after the mindful movement lesson, you might ask students to notice the sensations in their bodies when they are running on the playground or as they brush their teeth at home. It's great to tell them that there is no homework in mindfulness, and this is an invitation to become a mindful investigator in their own lives. Then they can remember to bring back their findings to the next class.

Closing Mindful Moment

At the end of the session, you can again lead a short mindfulness practice. This may just be a few mindful movements or a minute of belly breathing. Sometimes a mindfulness class will bring students to a very open state, and you want to make sure that transitions are not too abrupt. Let them know that you will be transitioning but they can stay connected to their attention, bodies, and hearts. You might say, for example, that you hope that these practices are helpful in their lives and that all the practices they have done can bring greater mindfulness into our whole world.

Mindfulness-Based Curriculum

✳

Having already learned our own mindfulness practices and how to embody them in our youth-based settings, it is now time to explore the wealth of mindfulness-based lessons we can offer to our students. You can begin to offer specific lessons using the layout from the previous chapter to help students integrate the practices. We will explore mindfulness-based lessons that help cultivate embodiment, attention, heartfulness, and interconnectedness.

These lessons are presented in a specific progression because some lessons are best practiced before others. It can be particularly important to begin with embodiment, helping students feel comfortable and engaged before trying to make them sit still and quiet. Cultivate a secure base with of embodiment and attention before leading students into the realm of the heart. Finally, the interconnection lessons help students integrate their inner practices into their outer lives.

Embodiment: We begin with embodiment lessons to gain the language of our physical sensation. Students need to feel safe and secure in their bodies before they can truly learn, collaborate, and gain emotional regulation. We begin by supporting the students to feel comfortable, connected, and relaxed in their bodies.

Focused attention: Once students learn the language of their bodies, they can begin cultivating their attention. We work with various sensory phenomenon, such as the breath and sound to anchor and stabilize attention. These practices cultivate the capacity to focus on schoolwork and other activities, but this attention is also the key building block for emotional regulation and responsible decision making.

Heartfulness: Once students have an understanding of the language of their bodies and how to anchor their awareness, they can learn how to identify and feel emotions in their bodies. Students learn to regulate difficult emotions by bringing kind awareness to these feelings. Students also learn to feel and strengthen beneficial emotions such as joy and compassion.

Interconnection: Once students have become mindful of their bodies, minds, and hearts, they can integrate their awareness into everyday life. They can learn to work with everyday distraction, frustrations, discomforts in the body, and other inevitable difficulties. Students can also bring compassion, forgiveness, and gratitude into action.

The 16 foundational mindfulness lessons that follow have been laid out in a progression that works well in classrooms and other youth-based settings. When presenting a new lesson, it is helpful to give at least 20 minutes for elementary students and at least 30 minutes for middle and high school students. There is a basic lesson layout in this section that is helpful to follow to support the integration of the new practices.

Once these lessons have been learned, you can weave the practices into the everyday experience of the class. You can open each day with some mindful communication, use mindful breathing for transitions, and encourage mindful focusing before tests. It is most important to gain a solid foundation with all the lessons and then learn how to work them into teachable moments throughout the day.

It's also wonderful to bring these practices into your lesson subjects. Whenever I lead five-day or year-long teacher trainings, I'm awed by the lessons teachers come up with. I have come up with scores of mindfulness lessons and still when I train teachers they come up with new ways to help kids develop attention and compassion that I have not thought of. Science teachers make up remarkable observational experiments to develop mindfulness through biology or physics lessons. Language teachers construct gratitude lessons through using compassionate language. Each teacher is an expert on their subject and their students.

For several years I worked with the organization Mindful Schools, training new facilitators to teach our curriculum in classrooms throughout the Bay Area in California. New facilitators would shadow me, and I taught the lessons over a course of several months. I must admit that I wasn't very good at this job of training teachers in the exact sequence of lessons. After the 15-minute lesson I would walk into the hall with the assistant facilitator and they would say, "That was great! But weren't you supposed to be leading a lesson on mindful listening?" The problem was that I would continually walk into the room with the intention of leading a particular lesson but would notice how the students were all talking about a fight that had just happened on the playground or some other particularly charged experience. I would shift course and lead a lesson about distraction, emotional regulation, anger, or some other practice tailored to the situation at hand.

The usual step-by-step curriculum progression didn't seem

to fit with the mindful paradigm of responding to the direct needs of the classroom in the moment. Instead, I was modeling how to cultivate a toolbox of lessons and interventions that could be used within a classroom once the teacher had mastered the lessons and modalities.

You can use the following lesson sequence, and you can also look at these lessons as a toolbox to construct your own mindful classroom and mindfulness lessons. You can use the sample scripts and lesson layouts as training wheels that will help you navigate fluidly. Eventually I invite you to construct your own lessons, progression, and language.

Embodiment Lessons

※

There is only one time and place in the entire universe where we can learn mindfulness, and that is here and now in our bodies. To open our eyes and truly see the world without all of our assumptions getting in the way, we first must feel comfortable in our own skins. The tool with which we begin exploring our inner world is our awareness, and the vehicle in which we learn is our body. We begin by learning the language of our sensations.

Helping students feel safe and secure in their bodies should be a top priority. If students don't feel comfortable, they will easily get distracted, act out, and have difficulty learning. All teachers know how distracting and difficult one dysregulated child can be in a class. We often feel like there is no time to spend creating a nourishing and supportive environment for our kids, but when we consider the amount of time that is lost trying to herd the attention of students back again and again to the topic at hand, we may realize that devoting special time to stabilizing and grounding our students, even if it takes half the class, is worthwhile in the long run.

We spend so much time these days worrying, that when we close our eyes we're swamped in the mess of our daily thoughts. To initially clear out some of that mess, we can begin with some simple movements and exercises in breath and awareness.

When there is a lot of frenetic energy in a classroom, it is important—imperative even—to meet the kids where they are. Instead of trying to tamp down the energy, which often makes it more intense, invite your students to do some relaxing and engaging movements and progressively bring them into stillness. The following embodiment lessons can be used to introduce even the most boisterous class into gaining awareness of their breath and their bodies.

Language of the Body

The language of sensation in the body is the foundation of our mindfulness. In our later lessons, it can allow us to become aware of the language of the mind and the heart. The first step for all students in learning the language of the body is introducing them to an exploration of their raw physical experience. We can imagine our own bodies as a foreign country we're visiting, one where we need to learn both the language and the landscape.

Often when I ask students and adults, "What are you noticing right now in your bodies?" they don't exactly know how to answer. With these embodiment lessons we and our students will learn to identify our physical sensations. We can experience pleasant, unpleasant, and neutral sensations, all of which we can learn to approach with a sense of calm inquiry.

Many curricula talk about teaching students alternate ways of dealing with anger and other difficult emotions. Somatic instructions, like the ones that follow, can help students learn how to identify these emotions in their bodies and transform them. Our emotions are experienced physically in our bodies; where else would we feel them? To cultivate lasting impulse control, emotional regulation, and attention, we need to begin by learning the language of our bodies. In doing so, we help our students feel relaxed, safe, and at home in their skin.

Learning Objectives

- Fostering a base of safety and centeredness in the body through familiarization and direct sense awareness.
- Building attention in the present moment with physical experience as a base.
- Building an understanding of the physiological experience to use in future exercises, such as attention building and emotional regulation.
- Cultivating equanimity and kindness to self and acceptance of pleasant and unpleasant sensations.

Preparation

One of the wonderful things about mindfulness is that you need nothing but your mind, your heart, and your body. You can open to awareness anywhere, and no props are required. For the following practice it is ideal for students to be sitting on the floor or in chairs. This practice can be done indoors or outdoors. An ideal space is one that feels safe and enjoyable with minimal distractions, and finding the safest and most inspiring space is important. If you plan to use them, make sure students have their mindfulness journals nearby so they can reflect quietly after the assignments.

Things to Remember

It is important to stay cognizant of the possibility of eliciting strong emotional responses by opening a child's awareness to sensations that may feel scary or uncomfortable. As we've discussed, the safety children feel in these practices can trigger painful memories or feelings. If a child has a difficult emotional experience, maintain a caring and attentive presence and support the student in recognizing where they are by grounding and reorienting them to the sensory world around them. In other words, they are here and now, not there and then.

Children often don't have a language for their sensations, so be patient in your exploration of cultivating sensation language. Let the students describe the experiences in their own ways rather than offering multiple choices. Let them come up with metaphors, images, and other creative ways to describe their experiences. If they are having trouble naming sensations, give examples of what they may be feeling, so that they can learn to identify the experience.

Sample Script: Sensation Exploration

Let's say you were going to another country—maybe India, China, or Mexico. You would need to learn the language and the customs to get around. Today we are going to take a journey of awareness in the country of our bodies. To get around, we need to learn the language of sensations and feelings. When we learn the language of our bodies then we can relax more easily, we can have more control over our reactions, and we can build our body skills for anything we do. When we are more aware of our bodies, we will be better at sports, dancing, skateboarding, playing guitar, and anything else we use our bodies for.

*To learn the language of our bodies, let's begin by
raising one hand and then letting our eyes close. Since
you cannot see your hand, how do you even know it is
there? What sensations do you experience in your hand
now? Let's create some more sensations so that we can
feel all the various sensations that a hand can feel.*

First, blow on your hand. What was that like?

Now shake your hand around.

Now give it a little massage.

*Now try touching your chair, your pants, or other
textures.*

*With each different movement, notice which sensa-
tions are there. Is there heat or cold, heaviness or lightness, pain or pleasure? There are so many different
things one hand can feel.*

Give the students plenty of time with each experience as
well as a chance to share which sensations are present. Again,
there is no such thing as a wrong answer. We are helping the
students grow a vocabulary for all of the various sensations
that can be felt.

Once they have a better understanding of the sensations
that are present, you can lead them into a journey through
exploring their whole bodies.

Sample Script: Body Scan

*Now that you know the language of the body, you can
take a trip through your inner landscape. You can
begin by getting your mindful body on, sitting up tall*

and proud, and simultaneously letting your body be relaxed and calm. Notice again what your right hand feels like. Can you feel each finger separately, the palm, and the whole hand? Remember that you are not trying to find anything specific, just noting whatever sensations are here right now. Now shift your attention to your left hand and notice the sensations there. Now see if you can become aware of both hands simultaneously. How do they feel the same and how do they feel different?

Now bring your attention down to your right foot. What sensations do you notice in your right foot? Can you feel the toes, the sole, and the whole foot? Now see if you can become aware of the other foot. Let's become aware of both feet at once. Now we can move our attention up to our hearts.

In the same way we were feeling our sensations in our hands and feet, how does your heart feel? Do you notice warmth, heaviness, fluttering, or anything else?

For a moment, see if you can feel both hands, both feet, your heart, and the rest of your body all at the same time. Notice if you can feel your whole body like a big beehive of sensations.

When you're ready, slowly open your eyes and bring your attention to the room. What did you notice?

Again give the students time communicate about what they felt in their inner exploration.

In classrooms you can often have children simply sitting in a circle doing this, but if space allows it can also be very beneficial to have them lie down. There are many body scan practices in which you lie down and progressively move through the body, noticing every part. You can also do this as a progressive relaxation where the students bring awareness to each body part on an inhale and then relax that area on the exhale. Moving through the entire body, usually from feet to head or vice versa, and consciously relaxing every part can lead to a deep state of rest.

Dialogue

For students sixth grade and up you can share a teaching story, a quote, or a prompt for a discussion on learning the language of the body. Follow the council structure and guide a discussion on the importance of becoming aware of the body. You could share Jim Rohn's quote, "Take care of your body. It's the only place you have to live." You can open up a rich discussion with this quote or any other one that reflects on the miraculous experience of having a human body.

> 'Tis in ourselves that we are thus or thus.
> Our bodies are our gardens to which our wills are gardeners.
>
> —William Shakespeare, *Othello*

Journaling Prompts

- Drawing: Draw a picture of your favorite part of this exercise.
- Writing: List all the sensations you feel in your body.

- In what ways do your hands feel different than your feet?
- How could becoming more embodied help you?

World Discovery

For world discovery in this exercise, you might say to students something like: "There is no homework in mindfulness. There is only the awareness that we carry from our lessons back into our lives and back into the world. This is why I like to call this section World Discovery.

"Some people say they are so embodied that they can feel atmospheric changes in their bodies so that they know when it is going to rain. As you walk out of the classroom see if you can continue to notice the sensations in your body. Notice what it feels like when you walk outside, when you play a game, when you take a shower, and when you lie down to sleep.

"Many people report that doing the body scan before they go to bed helps them relax and fall asleep. Try your body scan when you're going to sleep and when you wake up in the morning. See what you find."

Age and Stage

This exercise is applicable to any age group, but remember that the language will need to be adapted to suit the age group you are working with.

K–5: For elementary age students, this practice can take from 10 to 20 minutes. You can explore this lesson again and again sitting in a circle, or you can have students explore the sensations of their bodies at different times of the day in different activities. Inviting children back to their direct physical experience throughout the day offers them a home base to come back to.

Younger students will enjoy this practice if it is done playfully and as an inner body adventure. For example, you could have them imagine they are going in a submarine trip to investigate the sensations in their bodies, or use another adventure scenario.

Grades 6–12: For middle and high school students, this lesson can last anywhere from half an hour to a full hour. The lesson has students sensing particular parts of the body. Adolescents can have a more in-depth discussion about the experience of different sensations as pleasant, unpleasant, and neutral. Teenagers will be able to reflect on the ways they are in relationship to their sensations. Teenagers may be more interested in imagining they are scientists investigating the subtle cellular vibrations in the body.

Playing Mindfulness

Depending on the age group and population you are working with, you can use appropriate characters to inspire them around becoming more embodied. For little kids you may evoke Kung Fu Panda or a ballet dancer. For older kids you could talk about famous sports stars or pop stars who are good dancers. Explain to students that you are going to "play" mindfulness and that it is a game where you learn a lot about your own mind, breath, and body by linking your breathing to various movements.

When you lead this practice you will notice that you begin with fun external movements, and by the end, the students are focusing very deeply inside of their own bodies, noticing subtle movements and stillness. Instead of trying to get them to be still when that may be outside of their range of possibility, we slowly bring them to a place where it is within their range of possibility.

Students love to come up with their own movements, and you can extend this game for a long time, having students make up elephant breaths, princess breaths, and anything else they invent that has a good movement with the inhale and exhale. It is always helpful to begin with these fun, playful movements and then slowly make smaller and smaller movements until the students become aware of the subtle movement of breath within their bodies when they are still.

Learning Objectives

- Playing mindfulness introduces students to mindful breath awareness.
- The practices help cultivate attention by focusing awareness on the breath with body movements.
- The movements support the students to experience connection and aliveness in their bodies while also enhancing their capacity to relax and be centered.
- Through progressive practices students learn to go from fun external movements to internal stillness.

Preparation

It is important to make sure there is enough room for big movements where students can swing their arms without hitting each other. The movements are ideally done standing up so the students can make a full-body movement. If the class is too rambunctious, these movements can be done sitting in chairs or on the floor. For students with disabilities, these practices can be done subtly by simply lifting the hands or turning the head.

Sample Script: Spider-Man Breath

Has any one ever done the Spider-Man breath? No? Everyone breathe in and pull your hands in toward your chest and when you breathe out let your arms shoot out like Spider-Man shooting his webs. Let's do that a few times.

Now let's do the dolphin breath. Every time you breathe in, curve your arms up like a dolphin jumping out of the water and then bring your arms down as you breathe out. Let's do that a few times.

Now let's do the crocodile breath. Every time you breathe in, open your arms like the jaws of a crocodile and every time you breathe out let them drop. Let's do that a few times as well.

Now we can do a few butterfly breaths, where you let your wings open on the inhale and close on the exhale.

Now let's lift our shoulders up really tight when we breathe in and then as you breathe out let them fall and totally relax. Let's do that a few times.

This time let's be totally still without moving a muscle. When you breathe in and out, see if anything moves. Even though you're trying to be totally still, see if there is any movement. Did you notice anything?

Dialogue

Having gone from big movements to subtle awareness of movements within a still body, you can ask students, "What movements do you notice in your body when you are trying to be totally still?"

If students cannot come up with anything, you can always prompt them with questions such as, "Did you notice your shoulders moving, your belly, your chest?" Often the class has a palpably different feeling after these practices; there's a more relaxed and balanced sense. Since they've already done the language of the body lesson, you can ask what they are feeling in their bodies. Whatever the effect on the class, you can ask, "How does your body feel after doing the mindful movements?"

Journaling Prompts

- Drawing: Draw your favorite animal breaths.
- Writing: How does breathing in feel different from breathing out?
- When you are totally still what movements do you notice in your body?
- Can you think of some other movements where you could breathe in with your body one way and breathe out another?

World Discovery

"You can take these mindful breaths with you wherever you want. The next time you feel stressed or worried, try breathing in and tightening up your shoulders and then when you breathe out you can relax and let it all go. Do that a few times, and then just see if you can be still and feel the movement of breath in your body.

"See if you can come up with some more mindful movements. You could think of other animals and imagine the ways they would breathe in and out and practice that, or you could just make up some fun breathing stretches. Next time you come in to class we can share our mindful movements with each other."

Age and Stage

Students of all ages are well served by beginning mindfulness with breathing that is linked to movements. K–5 students enjoy the playfulness of animal movements and other games. Before doing attention lessons, the mindful movements are often ideal tools for inviting breath and stillness without prematurely trying to get students to be still and quiet.

Sixth–12th-grade students will engage with the movements without needing the games. A good way of engaging older students is explaining the benefits to sports, dancing, or any other skill they want to develop. The script is aimed at younger students but there are many mindful movement practices that can be used for teenagers. Qigong, tai chi, yoga, and many martial arts movements are affective in helping older students connect with their bodies.

Mindful Movement

Once we have become aware of sensations in the entire body, we can explore our sensations as we move. It's great to begin with simple movements; any everyday movement will do. Have students raise their hands in slow motion, tie their shoes in slow motion, or scratch an itch in slow motion—any kind of activity that's done so often it becomes automatic. From these simple movements we progress to becoming aware of larger body movements.

Learning Objectives

- The practice supports coordination and attentive body awareness.
- Becoming aware of the body in motion teaches children about their physical boundaries and the boundaries of others.
- Students can cultivate and enjoyment and appreciation of the subtle movements of their bodies.
- The practice can develop patience and anchored somatic attention.

Slow Motion Pick Up

Preparation

Depending on your space and your students, you will need to gauge which movements are possible. Wherever you are, you can have the students do simple movements such as tying their shoes in slow motion. To get up and practice mindful walking, the class will need to feel rather settled or they may begin tripping and bumping each other. You need to follow the pace of your class. Taking a mindful walk in nature can be a beautiful opportunity if the students are ready.

Sample Script: Mindfulness in Motion

Now that we are so aware of the sensations in our bodies, let's see what our bodies feel like in motion. Let's all

*pick up a pencil and write our names in slow motion.
We all probably write our names so many times in one
day that we do it on autopilot. Let's slow down so much
that we notice every movement, every touch of the pencil on our fingers, and the weight and touch of the pencil on the page. What was that like to be so slow and
aware?*

*Now that you can be aware of your smaller body
movements, you can actually become aware while
you're walking. To begin we can do a slow-motion
stand-up. Before you stand you may notice your muscles and body getting ready. Your body is an amazing
machine with muscles, bones, tendons, and a nervous
system that sends messages to all of these parts.*

*As we slowly stand up, see if you can be aware of
every tilt, every bend, and every muscle contracting
and relaxing. What was that like to stand up so
slowly?*

*When you were a baby, you didn't know how to walk,
and now we do it so much you don't even have to think
about it.*

*Let's begin by lifting one foot and breathing in and
then letting the foot fall as we breathe out. Just standing
in place, notice how your body feels as you breathe in
and out, lifting and dropping your feet. When you're
ready we'll walk around the room in a circle, making
sure we don't touch anyone else, feeling our feet rise
and fall. We can feel the ground beneath us and our
bodies moving back and forth. Now come back to your
original place. What was that like?*

As always you need to gauge your classroom. Some classes will not be able to walk around the room without causing a ruckus. With these students you can just have them walk in place, noticing their movements.

Dialogue

"How many of you have ever heard of something called 'being in the flow' or 'being in the zone'? Many sports stars, dancers, musicians, and others who are masterful at their art talk about a state called the 'flow' or being in the 'zone'. That's really a way of describing being totally mindful. We all experience this sometimes when we are jumping rope, walking quietly in the woods, kicking a soccer ball into the goal, or dunking a ball through a hoop. We can have the experience where all of our thoughts seem to fade into the background and we are absorbed into the sounds, smells, and sensations of our bodies. The more mindful we are of our bodies, the less our thoughts tie us up and the more we are free. And that makes us better at what we're doing, and able to have more fun at it. What does being in the 'flow' mean to you?"

Journaling Prompts

- Drawing: Draw a picture of yourself doing something mindfully in your life.
- Writing: What movements could you be aware of as you go through your day?

- How could being more aware of your movements help you?
- What stops you from being aware of your body?

World Discovery

After a mindful movement class, you can invite students to become aware of their mindful movements in everyday life. A good way to do this is to have them pick a mindful moment. Students choose an everyday movement like brushing teeth, opening the front door, practicing guitar, or stopping at a traffic light (for teenagers). When they choose their mindful moment they are instructed to try to notice every time that moment happens in their daily life and be as aware as they can be during that moment. If they have decided to become aware every time they open the door, they will try to feel the cold metal of the doorknob, for instance, and the sensations of their twisting wrist every time they turn the knob. These reminders help the students cultivate a continuity of their mindfulness practice so that they can extend it into daily life.

Age and Stage

Young children get a lot out of learning to do everyday tasks in a slow and meticulous way. K–5 students may have difficulty walking around the room without getting distracted, but keeping their attention on tying their shoes or writing their name in slow motion will be very productive. Students will enjoy slow body movements, as well as slow-motion walking or crawling, if this seems doable without the class losing attention.

Sixth–12th can gain a great deal from taking everyday tasks and bringing full attention to them. It can be helpful to explain how these practices can support them in their lives. They can use these exercises as training for other aspects of their lives. For older students mindful walking can be a wonderful way to cultivate attention. For some students sitting still is too uncomfortable; for these students, mindful walking is ideal.

Mindful Eating

When we eat mindfully, we gain a new way of relating to the experience of eating and to small everyday objects. Generally, we eat without bringing much awareness to the process. Our intention in this practice is to become aware of the great pleasure and beauty that can be experienced in a normal daily experience.

This is by no means just a practice of bringing awareness to taste, it is a full sense-based experience during which we explore our sense of touch, smell, hearing, sight, and taste. The mindful eating practice can help us and our students bring full sensory awareness to everything in our lives, whether it is eating breakfast or putting on our shoes.

Learning Objectives

- Enhance sense awareness and somatic presence.
- Cultivate gratitude and appreciation of the moment.
- Heighten attention and attunement skills.

Preparation

The ideal foods for this practice are small, tasty, and natural. A raisin, apricot, tangerine, or other similar fruit will do. Chocolate or other candies seem to be distracting and children have a harder time focusing. You will need two raisins for the exercise (since they are so small) or one tangerine.

Be sure to find out if there are children with food allergies in your classroom. Remember that some children might not like raisins and may have very particular food interests. If you know this about your students, you can choose and provide an alternative. Remember to wash your hands and all students' hands before you begin.

Sample Script

Today we are going to learn how to be mindful of something totally new. It's something we do all the time, and it can be really enjoyable, but often we are not mindful as we do it and miss the chance to enjoy it even more. What we are going to do is mindful eating, and to practice we will each get two raisins. When I put them in your hand, you can begin by looking very closely at them as if you were a scientist looking at them under a microscope. Now make sure not to eat the raisins yet. Remember, first we are being mindful scientists, looking at every color, shape, and form.

Hand out two raisins to each student. Often you can enlist a few children to help you pass them out. Let them look at the raisins for a minute, possibly recommending holding the raisin up to the light or seeing if the two raisins look similar or different.

What do you see?
Now let's give it a good smell. Hold it near your nose

and take a sniff with your eyes closed. What did that smell like?

Now let's close our eyes and rub the raisin between our fingers. What do you feel?

Great. Now let's see what the raisin has to say. You have probably never heard what a raisin has to say before, have you? Hold the raisin between your fingers and bring it up next to your ear, then roll it between your fingers with your eyes closed and see what you hear. To do this we need to be totally silent.

You probably never got to know a raisin so well. Now is the moment we have been waiting for. When I say so, we will slowly begin to eat our first raisin. In slow motion we will bring the raisins to our mouths and put them on our tongues. We will close our mouths, but don't chew yet, just roll it around in your mouth and see what it feels and tastes like. Let's get our mindful bodies on for this and close our eyes so we can really focus on the raisin. Ready, set, go.

Now let's take one bite at a time. Every time you bite, stop for a few seconds to taste and enjoy. Remember to feel the way your tongue and your jaw move. Chew very slowly, and when you're done chewing mindfully, feel the way you swallow the raisin.

Dialogue

To initiate a discussion you might say something like, "Usually when we eat raisins we just throw a bunch in our mouths really quickly and chew them so fast we hardly get a chance to taste them. We just ate two raisins and really gave them our attention. When we do this, we experience so much taste and so much enjoyment. It's like there was a whole world in one little raisin. Imagine if you ate an ice cream cone this mindfully. How do you think your life would be different if you paid this much attention to everything?"

You can do a council practice with teaching stories and quotes about fully experiencing their lives.

> *To see the world in a grain of sand, and to see heaven in a wild flower, hold infinity in the palm of your hands, and eternity in an hour.*
>
> —William Blake

Journaling Prompts

- Draw: Draw a picture of what it looks like inside your mouth when you're eating.
- Writing: How does eating mindfully feel differently from the way you normally eat?
- What else would you like to eat mindfully?
- What are some other things in your life that would be better if you slowed down?

World Discovery

"Every time you have something to eat, you can eat mindfully. You don't have to eat slowly to be mindful, you can just focus on the food you're eating and really pay attention to each bite. Imagine eating a piece of pizza, drinking a glass of your favorite juice, or eating a cookie this mindfully. Often we get something we really like eating but then while we're eating it we're thinking of other things or talking to people and not getting to really enjoy our food. So practice mindful eating over the next few days when you're eating or drinking something you like, and really focus on the taste. Enjoy."

Age and Stage

K–5 students enjoy the sensory experience of mindful eating, and younger kids love sharing what they smell, feel, see, hear, and taste. You can practice this game at every snack time for the first bite of snack if you like. It's a wonderful way to get students to slow down and enjoy their food. Take time with each sensory exploration and remember to remind younger children not to eat their raisins immediately when they get them.

Sixth- through 12th-grade students can use this practice to attune their senses and focus their attention. Students can get into the subtleties of noticing their mouths beginning to salivate even before they are eating and noticing the way the mouth moves when it chews. This practice can be done again and again as a means to cultivate embodiment and attention.

Attention Lessons

✻

Think of how many times your teachers and parents told you to pay attention as a kid, and then try to remember how many times they actually showed you how. To excel at reading, math, science, art, music, sports, or any endeavor, the ability to pay attention is crucial. Everyone wants to be able to pay attention, but sadly our education system has rarely incorporated the tools for actually developing these skills.

Instead of being controlled by our distracted thoughts and desires, the mindful attention practices set forward here help harness the wild mind. Once the mind is focused, it becomes a great ally at the command of our still and balanced awareness.

When students don't know how to pay attention or regulate their emotions, they easily fall into distracting behavior, often out of sheer frustration. All too often their distracting behavior may lead us to think that they're "just looking for attention" or intentionally being obstinate. As teachers, if we can offer these students the inner resources that they are lacking rather than penalizing them over and over, they have a much greater chance of thriving.

When talking about attention, it is crucial to use language that will inspire the students. Metaphors and stories are used to help them notice the distracted nature of their minds. You could ask students if they have ever had the experience where their eyes are scanning down the page of a book, but they are not actually registering the words, and then they have to read the page all over again. Once you have described attention and distraction, you can ask the youth themselves about what they wish they had better attention for. Once you have engaged them as participants in their own development, you can offer some basic explorations.

Anchor Breath

Anchor breathing is a core lesson in mindfulness practice. We call this practice the anchor breath because the breath can be an anchor, a home base, to which we can return any time. Though the waves on the surface of our lives may be tumultuous, there is a stillness that can be found down at the bottom of

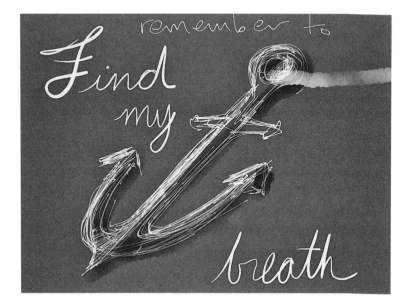

the ocean. Our anchor breath can be our connection to that deep calm inside our bodies.

One of the amazing things about the breath is that it is one of the few biological functions that is both conscious and unconscious. Luckily we don't need to think about breathing; breath effortlessly comes in and out of our bodies, oxygenating our blood at all times. If we want to, however, we can consciously control our breath. In this lesson we explore mindful breathing by simply witnessing the natural breath experience. It is important to let the children know that there is not a specific way that their breath is supposed to feel. The point of this exercise is to help them become aware of the sensory experience of breath however it is.

Learning Objectives

- Cultivating attention by using an awareness anchor.
- Finding stillness and relaxation within the body through breath awareness.
- Building an attention base for future emotional regulation lessons.

Preparation

For this exercise it is crucial to have a space with as few distractions as possible. It may be advisable to have students sit in seats with some space between them so that they will not be distracting one another. For younger students you can bring props to show them what a boat and an anchor is.

Sample Script: Anchor Breath, Step 1

Have you ever noticed how easy it is to get distracted when you are trying to pay attention to a teacher speaking or to a game you are playing? Your mind may even get distracted as I am talking now. The mind is kind of like a little puppy that keeps chewing up the pillows and making a mess on the floor. The puppy needs some training, just like your mind. Have you ever done something that you knew wasn't a good idea, but you couldn't help yourself? The practices we will explore will build your attention muscles with the strong focus that is needed to succeed at sports, playing a musical instrument, or taking a test.

Luckily there is a science to the mind. The more we relax and focus on what is happening right now, in the present moment, the more our minds naturally settle down. When we relax, we feel happier and we are better at doing everything we want to do. When we are stressed, our minds and bodies don't work as well, and we feel crummy inside. The more you focus on your breath and the other mindfulness practices, the better you will feel. You'll also be building your attention muscles so you can focus on your bike ride, your violin, or whatever you love doing.

Sample Script: Anchor Breath, Step 2

We can begin to cultivate our mindfulness by focusing on the breath. The breath is an incredibly useful tool in helping us calm the mind in emotionally charged situa-

tions and to pause and reflect before reacting. While there are many useful mindfulness practices, breathing mindfully is particularly useful because it can be used at any time and place throughout the day—when we are taking a test, waiting for a friend, or lying in bed at night. We call this breathing exercise the anchor breath because it can be used like the anchor of a ship to keep you grounded. Even if big waves of fear, sadness, or excitement come, you can use your anchor breath to calm your mind and body.

Take one hand and put it on your belly. See what you notice in your belly as you sit silently breathing in and out. What did you notice?

Now you can let your hand drop, and let's sit for a little longer, simply feeling the breath in our bellies. When you notice that you are thinking, gently bring your mind back to the breath. Whatever arises— thoughts, emotions, sensations—welcome them without judgment and then bring your attention back to the breath.

After about a minute, or longer if it seems like the students can sit comfortably, ask them to open their eyes. When the students are ready, ask them to share their experiences and to talk about how they feel right now, after the breathing practice.

With our questions, we are trying to elicit both the students' experiences of following their breath, as well as what they noticed in their distracted minds. You could ask:

What did you notice inside and around you as you began to practice mindfulness? How do you imagine that mindful breathing might help you? What chal-

lenges did you have in following the breath? How does your heart feel right now? What did you notice about your mind?

Dialogue

You can have a wonderful council on the storms in which we are so often caught in our lives, and how we can find calm with our anchor breath. You might begin a dialogue by quoting Oogway, from *Kung Fu Panda*, saying, "Your mind is like this water my friend, when it is agitated it becomes difficult to see. But if you allow it to settle, the answer becomes clear." You can ask what it is like to try to find a sense of calm in the stormy times in our lives by using Jon Kabat-Zinn's quote: "You can't stop the waves but you can learn how to surf."

Journaling Prompts

- Drawing: Draw a picture of an anchor that is still beneath the rough waves of the ocean.
- Writing: What ways did you find yourself getting distracted during your anchor breathing?
- How does your body feel after your mindfulness practice?
- What do you want to use your attention muscles for?

World Discovery

The anchor breath is a fundamental practice that we will return to again and again. You can ask students to practice the anchor breath for a few minutes every day and use it whenever they feel upset, feel nervous, or have any uncomfortable feeling. For example, you could say, "Before your next class, you may have a moment when you feel annoyed or even upset. When things happen that make you upset, it's like there's a storm in your life. When you notice this storm, remember your anchor breath so that even when the waves are crazy up above, there can be calm stillness under the waves and in your body. Notice what happens when you use your anchor breath during a storm, and then we can share with each other in the next class how our anchor breath worked."

Age and Stage

K–5 students need some more playfulness and guidance in this exercise. A 15- to 20-minute introductory lesson is ideal. Once students know the anchor breath, it becomes an indispensable practice to use in the beginning of every mindfulness class. This is also an important practice for transitions and whenever the class feels dysregulated. You can always tell the class or an individual student to remember their anchor breath.

I ask students if they know what an anchor is, and then spend some time making storm noises and saying that when a storm comes, your boat needs an anchor so it won't get blown out to sea. You can use props to show how an anchor is still beneath the waves even if the boat is getting blown around.

Then you can invite all the students to put one hand up and swoop it down to their bellies, asking them how the breath feels coming in and out. Some think it feels like a balloon getting bigger and smaller. You can say, "When you focus on how your belly feels as you breathe in and out, it's like you have an anchor inside you that is keeping you totally still."

Sixth–12th-grade students usually do not need much description of what an anchor is, but it's valuable to discuss what kinds of storms they experience in their lives and what it would be like to be able to have an anchor in troubling times. For an initial session it's ideal to have 30 minutes to an hour to offer this practice, and then have time for discussion and journaling.

This becomes a core practice for students to return to whenever they are feeling distracted or emotionally hijacked. With older students who can explore self-reflection to a greater degree, this is a foundational practice.

Things to Remember

Remember to have students become aware of their breath in their bodies. This is not a mental activity but a somatic exploration of how the breath moves in the body. We are anchoring our awareness to the sensations of the breath.

Sometimes students say that their bellies go out with the inhale and in with the exhale; sometimes students say the opposite. We are not trying to get kids to have a specific experience; we are helping them become expert investigators of their own bodies, hearts, and minds.

It is imperative when teaching these practices to remember that we are not offering them to make children more docile and malleable to our needs. These are tools offered to students for their own empowerment. We never force them on students. Therefore, it's important to present the profound benefits of the practices so they can decide to take the journey themselves.

Make sure to say the word *anchor* clearly. Sometimes kids hear the word *anger*, and practicing the "anger breath" is not what we are aiming for.

Mindful Listening

Often in our lives, we're thinking about so many things at once that we are not really aware of what is happening right in front of us. We have so much on our minds—things that already happened, things in the future—that we can easily miss the wonders of life all around us. If you can think back to what it was like to be a small child, you can probably remember how exciting even little things were. Watching a butterfly or to eating a strawberry could be ecstasy. As we get older, we lose some of our enthusiasm. This is because we get so familiar with what is happening around us that we forget to really notice and appreciate it. It's not that the butterfly is no longer beautiful or the strawberry is no longer as sweet, it's that we are no longer giving our full attention to life within and around us. It is almost as if we are sleepwalking. We think so much about what happened in the past and what we hope will happen in the future that we can be asleep to what is happening right now.

We can anchor our experience to the present moment in many ways. We can feel our breath, smell a flower, listen to sounds, or pay attention to anything else that is happening now. For this practice, we will be aware of the sounds that are all around us. When we listen to sounds, really listen to them, we don't have to do anything. We can just sit back and receive the waves of sound, almost as if we are sitting on a beach listening to the ocean waves hit the sand and recede again.

Learning Objectives

- Cultivating focused, present-moment awareness.
- Relaxing the mind and the body.
- Becoming aware of thoughts and working with distraction.

Preparation

This practice can be done indoors or outdoors, with few sounds or many. As you continue to teach this practice, it can be fun to find different sounds for the students to listen to. Ringing different types of bells, shaking rattles, and being in a place where there are plenty of sounds from nature can work well.

Sample Script: Mindful Listening

In this lesson, you will learn to open up your senses and experience the world in a richer and fuller way. We will practice mindful listening to cultivate our capacity to experience the world as it actually is, instead of the way we are expecting it to be. When we practice mindful listening, we will open up our awareness to whatever comes. The intention of this awareness

*exercise is to keep your listening ears open and stay
attuned to the sounds that surround you.*

*You can sit up straight and let your body be relaxed.
Let your eyes close, or softly look downward. Use your
anchor breath for a few moments.*

*Now you can begin to listen attentively to any sound
that arises. You can hear the sounds that are far away,
like airplanes, distant cars, or other sounds that you
can barely make out.*

*Now you can focus on more immediate sounds, such
as noise in the room or a bird chirping in the background.*

*If a thought comes into your head, let it rise up like
the sound of a car going by and then let it fade away.
Come back to listening.*

*Now bring your focus to the sound of your own
breath going in and out. Relax with the sound of your
own breath. You may hear your belly gurgling or other
inner noises. Continue to breathe deeply. When you are
ready, let your eyes slowly open and mindfully see the
world around you.*

Dialogue

When the class is ready, ask students to share their experiences and how they feel after practicing the exercise. You can
ask what noises they heard and what they noticed about their
minds as they tried to pay attention.

You can also share a teaching story or a quote to inspire a

conversation about listening and being fully in the present moment.

> *We have two ears and one mouth so that we can listen twice as much as we speak.*
>
> —Epictetus

> *Don't underestimate the value of Doing Nothing, of just going along, listening to all the things you can't hear, and not bothering.*
>
> —*Pooh's Little Instruction Book*, inspired by A. A. Milne

Journaling Prompts

- Drawing: Sounds are made of waves. Draw a picture of the ocean of sounds you are hearing right now.
- Writing: What are your favorite sounds to listen to?
- What do you notice about your attention when you try to stay focused on sound?
- How do you feel your emotions responding to each sound?

World Discovery

"Throughout the week, keep your mindful ears open and see if you notice any noises you usually miss. If you've been forgetting to really listen in your life, you may be amazed by all the amazing sounds all around you! Listen to the sounds and even see if you can find all the little pieces that each sound is made of."

Age and Stage

K–5 students will enjoy this practice when it is more playful. This is a good 5- to 10-minute lesson, or you could lead an hour-long musical listening class or nature walk. You can have kids listening to see how many different sounds they can hear. You can play different bells, and with their eyes closed, the students can try to guess which bells you were playing and in what order.

Young minds tend to wander away easily if there is no focus of attention, so ringing a bell that has a long duration of sound is helpful for younger students. Following the sound and then raising their hands when they cannot hear it any more helps them stay focused in the present.

Sixth–12th-grade students can spend five minutes and longer really focusing on sound. This is another way for adolescents to imagine building their attention muscles. It is important to help them remember that the moment they realize their minds are wandering, they can observe that they are no longer registering sounds, the moment they are listening to the thoughts in their heads, they are missing the music of the world. This is a great practice for opening and ending classes. Older students can begin to do a practice where they notice how their bodies respond to each sound.

Things to Remember

Listening is a core practice for students and can be used throughout the day, even for a single ring of a bell that students listen to. This can be a relaxing and regulating moment.

It is helpful to remind kids to *receive* the sounds instead of trying to *hear* them. They can relax as they listen, not needing to *do* anything.

Mindful Seeing

With mindfulness we use an anchor to stabilize our awareness. We can use the breath as the anchor, and we can use many other anchor points. One of the best anchor points for students to cultivate their attention muscles is using their eyes for mindful seeing. When we have students focus their eyes on a single spot, it helps them anchor their awareness. When they get distracted and their eyes move, it becomes very obvious to them they have spaced out or been distracted.

Learning Objectives

- The mindful seeing practice cultivates attention skills.
- This practice especially helps students to become aware of distractions.
- Students learn to return attention to a single-pointed awareness again and again.

Preparation

Classrooms often have posters, letters, and other pictures on the walls that can be used to focus the eyes. You can have all the students bring their attention to a single spot such as a ball or a dot on the wall. If you are outside you can have students look at trees, rocks, or any other stationary object.

Minimizing distractions from classroom visitors or other students during the lesson is helpful. Though we are working with distraction, it is best to begin with as few external distractions as possible.

Sample Script

To build our attention muscles we can use our mindful eyes. If we chose one spot to focus on, we keep our eyes stuck on that spot, and every time our eyes wander we can pull our attention back to that spot. Every time you bring your eyes back to that spot, it is like you are lifting weights and your attention muscles are getting stronger.

Look around the room and find a small image or object to focus on. Make sure it's not another person or something moving, and then let's hear from a few people what their spot is going to be.

Now that you have your spot, focus your eyes, and keep them glued to that spot for a whole minute.

Well done. What did you notice about trying to pay attention to your one spot?

Did your eyes get distracted?

Now let's play another seeing game. Let's get our mindful eyes on and look around to see if there is anything around that you have never seen before. Look as if you were a mindful detective, staying

totally quiet and still, examining the world by turning
your head. Did you notice anything you had never
seen?

Dialogue

If I can, I like to play a wonderful attention video of a group
of students passing a basketball back and forth. (You can find
this two-minute video at YouTube if you search for "Selective
Attention Test" by Daniel Simons and Christopher Chabris.)
The prompt for the kids is to count how many passes take
place. After the video, you ask how many passes the students
counted—and then ask if they saw the gorilla! When you play
the video again, everyone sees that a person in a gorilla suit
walks directly through the scene, but most students don't
notice this the first time. You can then have a conversation
around the question, "What else do we forget to pay attention
to in our lives, like not seeing the gorilla?"

Journaling Prompts

- Drawing: Look around the room and draw as many things
  as you can see.
- Writing: What in your life do you wish you could pay
  greater attention to?
- What are some things that distract you from paying attention?
- How can mindfulness help you?

World Discovery

"You can continue to build your attention muscles outside of mindfulness class. A few times a day, use your focusing eyes for a minute and try to hold your one-pointed attention. The more you do this, the better you will get at focusing. You can also become a mindful investigator by using your mindful eyes to look around your home, the school, and in nature to spot things you have never seen before."

Age and Stage

K–5 students enjoy this exercise, especially if it's turned into a game. You can invite students to say which types of animals have strong eyesight. Once they say hawks, cats, or any other animal, you can have them embody these animals and look as closely as they can at their object. Even kindergarten students can gain awareness of distractions through trying to focus on one spot and bringing their attention back when they realize they have wandered. The practice can last up to 15 to 20 minutes.

It can be helpful to have young students chose an object and then have a few students tell you what they have chosen so that you are sure they understand the directions.

Sixth- to 12th-grade students can use this practice to become aware of their distracted minds. You can say things like, "Have you ever noticed when you are reading the way sometimes your eyes go down the page, but you have not actually been taking in the words?" This gives them a common example of distraction with which they might identify. You can help adolescents understand that they are building their attention muscles every time they return attention to their visual point of awareness.

Things to Remember

Remember to tell students not to look at moving objects, especially each other. You don't want kids staring at each other during the practice.

There is a balance we want to help kids strike between focused and relaxed. If you see eyes bugging out of heads as they stare, remind them to have relaxed and focused eyes.

Once the practice has been taught, it is helpful to return regularly so that students can build their attention muscles.

Stream of Thoughts

Youth can gain a far greater awareness and mastery of their own thought processes than one may think. Middle school and high school students can learn to witness their thought patterns, and even kindergarten youth can learn to watch their passing thoughts. Witnessing thoughts is a crucial step in the process of regulating emotions and gaining impulse control. In the now-classic Stanford marshmallow experiment conducted by Walter Mischel in the 1960s, we see the profound import of being able to watch our own thoughts without reacting to them. In this study, researchers put a child in a room and gave him one marshmallow, then told the child that they would give him another marshmallow if he could sit there without eating his marshmallow until the researcher got back. The agony of the 10 minutes that follow can be seen on YouTube videos: children nearly pulling their hair out with anticipation. It turns out that when researchers checked in on the students 5, 10, and more years later, they were able to predict with incredible accuracy which students would exhibit addictive behaviors and even how well students would do on standardized tests. The effect of impulsivity on a child's life is immense, predicting criminality, drug abuse, and levels of financial success.

If the entire future of a child's life is dependent on his or her level of impulsivity, it would make a great deal of sense to figure out whether impulse control can be taught. This is exactly what we are doing with our attention practices. When you have an anchor for your awareness, it is far easier to control your impulses. Dysregulated children do not want to be dysregulated. Every child would rather have two marshmallows than one. If we have been strengthening our attention muscles, when the frenzied mind arrives (and it will), we can work to stabilize our awareness and watch the storm pass. Just imagine how many youth could end up forgoing their dangerous behaviors and focusing on what is really important to them.

The following practice works well for every age group. It gives students an increased ability to witness their own thoughts, helping create some space between thoughts and actions. This is the space between a thought like, "I don't like that guy," and the action of hitting him. In this brief reflective moment, students can get some objectivity about their thoughts; consequently they can make better decisions. If we can help kids expand this space, we are giving them a better opportunity to self-regulate.

Learning Objectives

- This practice cultivates self-reflective thinking.
- With self-reflection and awareness of thoughts impulse control is strengthened.
- Students gain an understanding of the effects of their thinking on their emotions.

Preparation

Once students have cultivated the ability to stabilize their awareness with the anchor breath, they will be ready to give this practice a try. Students need to be familiarized with this capacity to bring the attention back to an anchor before they will be able to witness their thoughts. You will need to make sure the room is quiet and has as few possible disruptions as possible.

Sample Script: Stream of Thoughts, Step 1

Imagine your brain is like this room we are sitting in. Now let's imagine we pushed all the chairs, desks, and papers out the windows. Imagine your brain is like a big empty room. Now get your mindful body on and bring your awareness to your anchor breath.

Every time a thought comes into your empty mind, you can silently pop your hand up in the air and then put your hand down and imagine you're clearing the room again and coming back to your anchor breath.

You may have only a few thoughts visit you, or you may have a new one jumping through the door every second. What's important is that every time you notice a thought, you pop your hand up and then come back to your anchor breath.

Sample Script: Popcorn Thoughts, Step 2

Our thoughts are always moving like a stream. Imagine there was a stream in front of you with twigs and leaves

*floating down it. You could reach out and pick up some
of these twigs and leaves, or you could let them pass by.
This is the same way our minds work with thoughts.
Usually what happens is that we pick thoughts up out of
the stream. Let's say you have a thought about getting
ice cream after school. Maybe you pick that thought up
out of the stream and then add a bunch more thoughts
like, "will I get vanilla or strawberry?", or "the last time
I got an ice cream cone I dropped it and was so upset."
Pretty soon we are all wrapped up in thoughts of future
or past, and we are no longer aware of what is happening right now.*

*What we are going to do is to sit on the side of the
thought stream and whichever thought comes by, we
will just watch without picking it up. If you realize all
of a sudden you have picked a thought up unintention-
ally, that's fine, just return to your anchor breath and
let the thought go.*

*When we are using our anchor breath, we don't need
to push anything away, we can just stay centered on
our breath and watch the thoughts flowing by. You can
notice if the thoughts make you excited, scared, happy,
sad, bored, or something else. Whatever thought passes,
notice how it effects your body.*

Dialogue

You can have the students share their experiences of watching
the stream of thoughts. This makes an intriguing conversation
around witnessing the nature of our minds. You can say, "All

types of things come down the stream of thoughts, like the memory of an argument, planning your birthday, or worrying about a test. When each thought comes, how does it affect your body, your breath, and your emotions?"

You can also share quotes or stories that acknowledge the fact that we can witness our thoughts. I often tell students about the bumper sticker I once saw that said, "Don't believe everything you think."

Journaling Prompts

- Drawing: Draw a picture of a stream and then draw all of your thoughts like things floating down the stream.
- Writing: What types of thoughts do you find yourself picking out of the stream most often?
- Where do you think thoughts come from?
- What is happening when you are not thinking?

World Discovery

Once we have learned to witness our thoughts, we can do so whenever we want. Whether you are at the park or at home, you can watch your thoughts and decide what you want to do with them. If you have a judgment about yourself, or someone else, you can always take a moment to ask yourself, "Is this thought true?"

When we can witness our thoughts, we can find a greater sense of stillness and relaxation. Instead of just being caught in the storm of your thoughts, you can notice angry, excited, or sad thoughts and simply put them back in the stream. Suggest to students that they try to notice their thoughts wherever they are and work on witnessing them as passing objects in the stream.

Age and Stage

K–5 students can gain self-reflection with fun thought games. You can tell them, "Your mind is like a popcorn maker, but instead of making popcorn it makes thoughts. Every time a thought comes into your mind you can pop your hand up and then let it fall and clear your mind. Then pop your hand up again when another thought comes." These simple exercises offer young children the profound ability to become aware of their own thought processes.

Sixth- through 12th-grade students can become aware of their thinking process and go a step or two further. Depending on their age and capacity, students can learn to watch their thoughts and become aware of when they are grabbing or pushing them away. With this awareness, they can also witness which emotions arise when thoughts come. They may get excited by certain thoughts and angered by others. Once they can track this process, it gives them a high level of self-reflection and self-regulation.

Things to Remember

It is important to remind students that the point of mindfulness is not to get rid of their thoughts but to be conscious of them and notice the influence they have on us. The goal is greater awareness.

Remember not to judge specific thoughts as good or bad. Happy thoughts, disturbing thoughts, creative thoughts—whatever arises can simply be noticed as a popping thought.

Heartfulness Lessons

✾

With heartfulness we learn to identify healthy and destructive emotions so that we can properly tend to our inner world. We learn to water the seeds of compassion, love, creativity, joy, and understanding and at the same time we learn to work with the seeds of jealousy, anger, and fear that want to sprout. Ultimately, we acquire the skills to grow a healthy and beautiful inner ecosystem that can inspire and feed the outer world.

The attitude of mindfulness is an expansive perspective that accepts everything exactly as it is. It can seem like a paradox to be totally accepting while choosing specific states of being to nurture while neglecting others. In the perspective of mindfulness, we do not believe that there is such thing as a negative emotion. We do not label things as good and bad. Instead, we are attentive in our observations of which emotional states are constructive and which are destructive. We can see how dwelling in anger promotes disease in our bodies and conflict in the outer world. We can explore how our inner cultivation of kindness can soften our hardened hearts and promote intimacy with our friends and family.

To cultivate happiness, compassion, and gratitude, we can bring into our minds and hearts experiences that inspire these feelings. We reflect on the things that make us feel grateful and recognize within our bodies how gratefulness feels. We can then learn to generate this state so much that it becomes habitual. Meanwhile we can use our capacity to witness destructive thoughts and feelings without getting caught up with them. This practice helps students break out of destructive mental and emotional patterns while learning healthy responses.

We have already learned the language of sensation and witnessed the nature of the mind; we can now explore the emotional body, encouraging students to experience the emotions as sensations while letting their thoughts gently float down the stream.

Heartful Phrases

Speaking heartful phrases generates kindness for ourselves and others. When we say these phrases, we do not need to imagine that the person is receiving our wishes; the point is to cultivate the generosity and goodwill within ourselves. When we say "may you be happy," we are finding in our hearts the genuine care for others and ourselves.

Sometimes students will say, "I don't feel happy, so I don't want to fake it." This is a statement to honor, reflecting the student's desire for authenticity. Usually I will ask in return, "Do you *want* to feel happy?" Even if we don't feel happy at a particular moment, we can often get in touch with a desire for happiness. This desire for happiness is what fuels heartful phrases. We can genuinely say, "May I be happy," *especially* when we are not feeling good. It takes courage to care for ourselves in this way, and I see this courageousness transform classroom environments every day.

Learning Objectives

- Cultivating care and compassion for self and others.
- Focusing on positive states and emotions.
- Creating an empathic classroom.

Preparation

It is necessary to have learned the language of the body lesson and to have awareness of the stream of thoughts. Having an anchored awareness and an understanding of sensations in the body sets the foundation for students to gain a greater understanding of how emotions work.

It's also helpful to do these classes in a safe and contained space. Make sure to remind students that everything that is shared is confidential.

Sample Script: Heartfulness Send Out (K–5 Students)

Let's all give ourselves a big hug. Now that we are hugging ourselves, let's say some kind words to ourselves. "May I be happy." You can smile and let yourself feel so good right now. "May I be healthy." You can feel your body really strong and alive. "May I be safe." You can relax and know that nothing can hurt you right now. "May I be at peace." You can know that you are totally perfect exactly as you are. Are there any more things that you want to wish for yourselves?

Now let's open up our arms as if we are shooting our kindness out of our hearts to everyone in the classroom. Let's say, "May you be happy, may you be healthy, may you be safe, and may you be at peace." What else do you wish for your classmates? You can open up your arms even wider, as if you were trying to give a hug to the whole world. Imagine you are sending kindness all the way to China, Germany, and Mexico. "May the whole world be happy, may the whole world be healthy, may the whole world be safe, may the whole world be at peace." Are there any other wishes you want to send out to the world?

Sample Script: Sending Heartfulness (6–12-Grade Students)

Today we are going to focus on something a little differ-ent than sounds, breath, or sensations in our feet. We are going to bring our attention to our emotional body. Let's all get our mindful bodies on. We can start by thinking about a time when someone did something really kind for us. Maybe they got you a gift, or said something really nice, or maybe it was even your pet cuddling and playing with you. Once you get that memory in your mind, play it on repeat. Now become aware of how remembering this experience feels in your body. See what sensations are in your heart. If this is a good feeling, see if you can expand the feeling throughout your whole body, like pushing up the dim-mer on a light switch. See if that good feeling can course through your whole body. Now that you are con-nected to your heart, let's send some of this kindness to others. Picture the person who was so nice to you and then send them the following phrases.

"May you be happy." When we say this, we can pic-ture the person smiling, feeling happy and content with his or her life.

"May you be healthy." Imagine this person is strong,

*taking deep, healthy breaths and having no sickness in
his or her body.*

*"May you be safe." Now imagine this person relax-
ing, without needing to worry about anything, totally
protected.*

*"May you be at peace." Imagine this person in a state
of tranquility, with a focused mind and an open heart.*

*As you repeat the phrases, notice what your heart
and the rest of your body feels like.*

From this practice you can have students send heartfulness
to themselves using the phrases "May I be happy, " "May I be
healthy," "May I be safe," and "May I be at peace."

This is not an affirmation practice. We are not saying "I am
happy." Since we know that everyone wants to be happy, even
if they are not happy at that moment, we are inviting a truly
desired experience. We are kindly asking for ourselves and for
others what we really want.

Eventually, you can ask students to send heartfulness to
someone who annoys them. This forgiveness practice can be
deeply heart-opening and has the capacity to transform a classroom environment.

Dialogue

It is important to start by asking students how this practice
makes them feel in their bodies. Usually it creates positive feelings in the heart. If this is the case, it is important to ask students how they would like to use this heartfulness practice in
the future.

You can also ask what other positive wishes students have for themselves, for others, and for the world.

You might want to discuss quotes or stories, such as Roald Dahl's *The Twits*, where he says, "A person who has good thoughts cannot ever be ugly. You can have a wonky nose and a crooked mouth and a double chin and stick-out teeth, but if you have good thoughts it will shine out of your face like sunbeams and you will always look lovely."

Journaling Prompts

- Drawing: Draw a picture of happiness spreading around the world.
- Writing: How does heartfulness make you feel inside?
- What would the world be like if everyone was practicing heartfulness?
- What other kind wishes do you have for yourself and others?

World Discovery

"Try to begin by cultivating heartfulness for yourself. Every night before you go to bed and every morning when you wake up, say these four phrases to yourself. Really wish these qualities for yourself. Be kind to yourself. You will see how much you can change your whole day by using these phrases. It's like brushing your teeth every morning and night, but instead of spending time caring for your teeth and mouth, you're strengthening and taking care of your heart. Give it a try and see how it affects you."

Age and Stage

K–5 students seem to be the most comfortable when it comes to sending and receiving kindness. The younger students are, the easier it seems to be to open up their hearts. Students enjoy coming up with wishes to send to themselves and others, so it is a game they are happy to repeat regularly, like every morning or every afternoon. The younger children usually need less prompting and are happy to send kind thoughts to others and loving thoughts to themselves, even in front of others.

Sixth–12th-grade students, sadly, often don't think it's cool to be nice to themselves and others. When speaking to teenagers, you might find it helpful to say something like, "We all want to be happy, have people like us, and feel comfortable being ourselves. It's really sad that sometimes we think that to be cool, we need to be mean and not let people see who we really are. Heartfulness helps us be brave enough to get real and keep our hearts open."

Once older students learn to send kind and caring thoughts to themselves and people they care about, they can learn to send caring thoughts to those who annoy them or with whom they have had conflict. This becomes a practice of forgiveness and heart opening. This type of compassion practice can be framed as very courageous and powerful work.

Things to Remember

When inviting students to imagine someone to send heartfulness to, we need to be very particular. You can tell them to picture a person who is really nice to them and whom they see regularly. If you are not specific, they may chose someone who has passed away or who has hurt them in some way.

When entering into heartfulness practices, we may encounter painful and even traumatic feelings. It is imperative to have some trauma training for this. It is also important to have contact with collateral resources, such as school therapists.

Remember that there is no such thing as a negative emotion. Anything that comes up for a student is okay. If a student says that the practice makes her angry, this is just as good an exploration as if she says it makes her happy.

Roots of Emotions

Since we have learned the language of our minds and our bodies, we can now understand where emotions come from. When we get angry, sad, excited, or anything else, we usually begin to think a lot. If we are angry, we remember the bad thing that happened or fantasize about saying something mean in return. We often get trapped in a mental loop, either repetitively reviewing what happened in the past or wondering what we will do in the future.

Instead of being consumed by thoughts, we can work with our body sensations. Every time we have a circling thought, we can imagine that it is like a branch with leaves fluttering in the wind. You can put your arm up in the air and picture it like this branch of thoughts. If you track down the branch, down your arm, there is always a root of emotion in your body.

Every time you are scared, angry, worried, happy, you can track the emotions down into your body and see what it feels like. Whenever you have lots of thoughts, it means that there is a corresponding feeling down in your body.

The great thing about understanding this is that when you can identify the feeling in your body, you can work with it. Trying to get rid of thoughts is like trying to block the ocean waves; they just keep coming. When we go to the source of emotions

Roots of Emotion

we can learn to feel them in our bodies and work with them constructively. If you're feeling angry you can't fix it by thinking about it, but you can go right inside, feel the hot, tight, anger, and let the body sensations go. It will feel so much better than repeating the same angry thoughts over and over in your head.

Learning Objectives

- Learning to feel emotions directly in the body and letting them go.
- Emotional regulation and letting go of difficult emotions.
- Relaxation techniques and self-control.

Preparation

This practice can bring up emotions for students. Make sure that you are in a contained space and remind the class of confidentiality. It is necessary to have practiced the language of emotions lesson as well as the stream of thoughts lesson. You want students to already have a good grasp of how they feel their emotions in their bodies and to be able to witness their thoughts.

Sample Script: Vacuum Breath

The vacuum breath can help us relax and let go of stressful feelings really fast. Every single person— grown-ups, kids, teenagers, teachers, even the president of the United States—gets stressed sometimes. There are certain events that arise that create reactions inside us. Like when someone jumps out of a closet and scares you, your whole body would tighten up, you would probably take a quick breath, and then freeze.

It's easy to see that kind of reaction in the body, right? Well, other types of reactions happen all the time in the body, but we don't notice them as much. Maybe you get left out of something you wanted to do with your friends, or someone says something mean to you. Every time something like this happens, our bodies react in a certain way. If we feel angry, our anger may feel like tightness in our bellies or heat in our faces. When you feel sad, you may feel an ache in your heart or a heaviness in your body. No one likes to feel this way, but we don't know any ways to make ourselves feel better. With the vacuum breath we can find these unpleasant feelings, suck them up with our vacuum cleaner, and then let them go. So let's start.

First get comfortable in your mindful body and let's take three big mindful breaths together. Good. Now let's scan through our bodies to see where we may feel any stress or difficult emotions. As you go through your body, see if there's pain, tension, or uncomfortable feelings anywhere. Right now we are not trying to get rid of these feelings, we are just trying to notice them.

Starting at your head, see if there is any stress, any headachy sensations, any jumpy thoughts, or anything else that is uncomfortable. Then move down through your shoulders and arms to see if there is any tightness or stress there. Then make your way through your heart and belly, feeling any emotions or painful sensations. Then make your way all the way down through your body, through your legs, all the way to your feet. Did anyone feel any uncomfortable feelings or difficult emotions?

Now that we have noticed these uncomfortable feelings, what can we do with them? Luckily we have a vacuum in our bellies. When you breath in, you can imagine the vacuum in your belly sucking in all of the uncomfortable feelings you may have. Starting from your head, pull any headaches or annoying thoughts into the vacuum cleaner. Then move through your heart to suck up all the sadness or nervousness. Pull any tension or uncomfortable feeling from your arms, your legs, your entire body into your vacuum cleaner belly. Then hold the breath in the belly for three seconds. When you are ready, let all the air come out of your body and the hard feelings with it. Just like you were emptying all the dust out of the vacuum cleaner.

As you breathe all the air out, let your body totally relax. Let go. Then again take a good long breath, feeling any stress in your body and vacuuming it into your belly, holding the breath there for three seconds, and then relaxing with your out breath. Let's try this vacuum breath for a whole minute starting right now.

Dialogue

This exercise often creates a dramatic difference in the students' experience of the room. Let the kids share how it made them feel personally, as well as how the room may feel different from before.

Journaling Prompts

- Drawing: Draw a picture of what it looks like when you are releasing all the stress from your body.
- Writing: What uncomfortable emotions did you notice as you went through the body?
- How did the vacuum breath effect your body?
- When could you use this practice in your life?

World Discovery

Now that the students have experienced the vacuum breath, they can do it anywhere. Remind them that if they get angry at their sibling, or their parents won't let them do something they really want to do, or something really scary happens, they can try the vacuum breath. I tell students that it works better than anything else to calm me down quickly and release some of the hard feelings that I have sometimes. Have them try it out over the next few days and then share about it during the next mindfulness lesson.

Age and Stage

K–5 students can do a shortened variation of this practice. The visual of a vacuum cleaner in the belly pulling in all the uncomfortable feelings is helpful for them. The practice can be very beneficial for students and the whole class when there is a lot of stress in the room, before a test, or after an incident. When doing the body scan with younger children, allow only a minute or so to go through the whole body, exploring unpleasant feelings.

Sixth–12th-grade students can explore in depth the intricacies of how emotions can be felt as physical sensations. It can be extremely liberating for students to track their emotional thoughts into their bodies, where they can relax them and let them go. With older students, you can take time during the body scan to feel into each body area to notice stress, pain, and unpleasant emotions.

Things to Remember

The vacuum breath can open up a lot of energy and emotion in the body. As always, get some training in trauma and have resources available in case intense emotions arise. When emotions do arise, it can be a great opportunity to support the students and let them know that everything is welcome in the class and there are no judgments on emotions.

Remember to let the students know that the goal isn't to get rid of these feelings but to simply notice them just as they are. We are trying to become aware of the emotions and let them relax, but we need to be sure that we are not pushing them away.

Destructive Emotions

Once we have opened the door to our emotions, we can begin to work with difficult feelings as well as easy or pleasant ones. If we don't know how to navigate through emotions such as anger, sadness, and fear, they can be very destructive. Since we can assume that these emotions will visit our hearts at some point, we use heartfulness so that instead of getting disturbed when they arrive, we can learn and grow from the experience.

You can lead students through all types of inner journeys that bring out emotional experiences. We want to be careful not to bring up emotions that are too intense. Whenever strong feelings bubble up, we tell students that their anchor breath is right there to support them. You can get into wonderful conversations about how the emotions feel physically in their bodies. When students can feel anxiety as a shakiness in their heart and belly, or sadness as a heaviness and aching, they are empowered to work with those emotions. When you can feel your emotions as sensations and name them with language, then you can bring your heartfulness to difficult feelings and respond to them constructively.

Learning Objectives

- Building emotional intelligence.

- Cultivating emotional regulation by gaining awareness of emotions.
- Gaining understanding of how destructive emotions negatively affect self and others.

Preparation

This practice should come after learning the language of the body, anchor breath, and roots of emotions. Make sure students already have an anchor they feel safe to come back to. Again, it is imperative that you create an emotionally and physically safe space, everyone agrees to confidentiality, and outside resources are available.

Sample Script: Heartfulness Journey

Since we already know about our anchor breath, we have a base that we can come back to whenever we feel scared or uncomfortable. Everyone experiences fear, anger, sadness, and other difficult emotions now and then. Maybe someone says something mean to you on the playground, or you don't get something that you want. Everyday we all have experiences where we don't feel so hot. We can assume that these hard feelings will arrive. What's important is what we do when they knock on the door.

Let's all get our mindful bodies on and follow our anchor breath. When you feel settled, I'll take you on a little journey in your mind. Imagine we go out on the playground and are having a lot of fun with your favorite game. What does that feel like?

Now imagine that two kids right next to you start fighting over a ball. What sensations do you notice in your body now?

Come back to your anchor breath and stay with the breath until you can feel yourself relax.

Now imagine someone comes over and says something mean to you. Notice what that feels like in your body. Remember your anchor breath. You can notice the discomfort in your body and then come back to your centering anchor breath.

Now imagine someone comes over to you and says something really nice and maybe even gives you a big hug. What does that feel like in your body? Do you feel happy, safe, scared, whatever you feel is perfectly all right.

Dialogue

Invite students to share how each imaginary scene affected them. Remind them to share how they were affected in their bodies. If they say, "I felt sad," then invite them to explore what sadness feels like in the body. You can help them by asking where they feel the sensations in their bodies—in their throats or their eyes, for example—and what it feels like—if it is hot, tense, heavy, or achy, for example.

You can ask students to remember their favorite moment, close their eyes and picture it, identify how it feels in their bodies, and then share with everyone how it feels.

You can also share some inspiring quotes, poems, or stories

about difficult emotions or becoming aware of emotions in the body. Below you will find a quote and a poem that can prompt good discussion.

> *One ought to hold on to one's heart; for if one lets it go, one soon loses control of the head too.*
>
> —Friedrich Nietzsche

> *It is easy enough to be pleasant*
> *When life flows by like a song,*
> *But the man worth while*
> *is the one who will smile*
> *When everything goes dead wrong.*
> *For the test of the heart is trouble,*
> *And it always comes with the years,*
> *And the smile that is worth the praises of earth*
> *Is the smile that shines through tears.*
>
> —Ella Wheeler Wilcox

Journaling Prompts

- Drawing: Draw a picture of the happiest thing that you can remember, and as you draw see how you feel in your body.
- Writing: Which disturbing feelings come up most often?
- How do these emotions feel in your body?
- What places and situations in your life make you feel the best? How do they make you feel?

World Discovery

Now that your students know how to witness emotions in their bodies, they have an amazing tool they can carry with them wherever they go. Remind them that if they feel scared, sad, or anything else that's difficult or unpleasant, they can become aware of the feeling in their bodies and then do some mindful breathing. They can also begin to become aware of how they feel in different places and with different people. You can point out that they may realize that whenever they play with one friend they feel angry, and when they play with someone else they feel happy and relaxed. Explain that once they do this type of investigation into how their body responds to places and people, they can learn to choose experiences that make them happy.

Age and Stage

K–5 students enjoy going on an imaginary journey in their minds. You can set up all types of scenarios for them. Some teachers lead collaborative imaginary journeys though the jungle or outer space. They tell the students they are going on a safari and the students get to imagine another world together, choosing the adventure as they go. Bringing students back again and again to noticing what they are feeling in their bodies is what makes this a mindfulness practice. This practice helps young children to become aware of the emotions that arise in different situations and how to regulate their systems.

Sixth–12th-grade students can learn a great deal from this practice as well. Instead of imagining they are going on a safari, the metaphors can be more focused on imagining an experience they are frustrated with. When students can learn to witness the sensations that arise in difficult moments, they begin to gain control of their responses. This leads to some fascinating conversations for older students.

Things to Remember

When teaching students about destructive emotions, it is important to tell them time and time again that there is no such thing as a negative emotion. We are not trying to get rid of "bad feelings," we are learning to take care of our hearts in emotionally turbulent times.

Gauge your audience to see what they are emotionally capable of. The scenarios you set up are intentionally instigating certain emotions, but of course you only want students to feel what is appropriate. Create the scenarios very consciously and describe them clearly.

Generating Gratitude

What are you grateful for? This question invites a mindset that appreciates what the world has already offered us, rather than always looking at what isn't enough. Instead of thinking about how you wish the world was different, you can learn to look to the world with a reverence for that which has already been given. Each breath has been gifted by trees and plants. Our food is a gift from the plants and animals. When we look at the miraculous phenomenon of life, it can awaken gratitude, love, and compassion within us.

When we are compulsively thinking and striving to make our world different than it is, we miss the big and the little beautiful things right in front of us. We can overlook the people in our lives who are caring, the community that supports us, and the environment that keeps us alive. Many of us have difficulties in our lives, and we are not trying to overlook these. We may have very little money or food, or there may be a lack of caring people in our lives. Of course we want those who are being neglected to get more support and love. Beginning with gratitude can help us see what in our lives is beautiful, even if all we have is one nice teacher and one bowl of soup to enjoy. With one step of gratitude, we begin walking in the direction of compassion and happiness.

Learning Objectives

- Gratitude practice cultivates happiness and a positive mindset.
- Shifting attention from destructive thought patterns to positive thinking.
- Compassion for self and others built by focusing on gratitude.

Preparation

It is ideal to use this practice as a council dialogue. If possible get the group in a circle and use a talking piece.

Sample Script: Getting Grateful

Sometimes we forget all the things in our lives that we can be grateful for. It's like the rock at the top of pyramid that isn't aware of all the rocks below it is sitting on. We have so many ancestors who had to survive and fall in love and do so many things for you to come along. For you to be here, the sun has to keep rising every day to give life to the plants that we need to breathe and eat. There are so many people we don't even think of who clean the bathrooms we use, drive the food to the store where we buy it, and build the building we live in.

If we really take time to think about it, there's an

endless number of things to be thankful for. When we focus on the things we are thankful for, it naturally makes us more happy. When we are focusing on what we don't have and what makes us upset, we feel lousy. Today we will practice our gratitude and we can explore inside how it shifts our state of mind.

Let your eyes close and get your mindful body on. Feel your breath coming in and out of your belly. Once you feel calm, picture the person in your life who makes you feel the happiest. Get a picture of that person in your head, and then imagine they are sitting right next to you. How does it feel to have them so close?

Now picture your favorite food and imagine it sitting right in front of you. Picture the colors and the smells and see what your body feels like.

Now keep thinking of your favorite things and people in your life. Think of the things you are most grateful for. When you picture them, see how they make your body feel.

Now take a deep breath and let all the things you are grateful for go, and simply notice what your body feels like after gratefulness practice.

Dialogue

Gratitude practice in a group is especially meaningful and transformative. A group can begin every day by saying what they are most grateful for in their lives and end the day saying what they were most grateful for that day in class. This positive attention can totally shift the environment of a classroom.

It is also beneficial to help kids figure out what about themselves they are grateful for. They can name attributes within themselves that they like. It can also be wonderful for a class to do a spoken or written exercise where each student names what they are grateful for in every other student.

Here are a few quotes on gratitude that can be used to inspire discussion.

> *We can complain because rose bushes have thorns, or rejoice because thorn bushes have roses.*
>
> —Abraham Lincoln

> *Once a little boy sent me a charming card with a little drawing on it. I loved it. I answer all my children's letters—sometimes very hastily—but this one I lingered over. I sent him a card and I drew a picture of a Wild Thing on it. I wrote, "Dear Jim: I loved your card." Then I got a letter back from his mother and she said, "Jim loved your card so much he ate it." That to me was one of the highest compliments I've ever received. He didn't care that it was an original Maurice Sendak drawing or anything. He saw it, he loved it, he ate it.*
>
> —Maurice Sendak

Journaling Prompts

- Drawing: Draw a picture of yourself surrounded by all the things you are most grateful for.
- Writing: Write a list of the things in your life that you are most grateful for.
- What are some things, like the sun and the rain, that you need to live?

- What aspects about yourself are you grateful for?

World Discovery

Once students have been introduced to a gratitude practice, they can begin their own gratitude journal. The journal might be something they keep indefinitely or for a limited time, like a week or a month. Encourage them to make an entry every day about what they are grateful for. Sometimes they may be grateful for so many things, and sometimes maybe they will just be able to find a few. Tell them that if they can make at least one entry every day about what they're grateful for, they will see how it can brighten their whole day. At some point in the future, make time to discuss the things they've noticed abut themselves and the world since starting keeping the journal.

Age and Stage

K–5 students easily enter into both the visualization and sharing about what they are grateful for. This practice can be used every morning in a circle as a way to check in or in the afternoon as a way to share what they were most grateful for during the day. Weaving gratitude into the classroom creates an environment of appreciation and kindness.

Sixth–12th-grade students can engage in very interesting discussions about cultivating positive mind states as a result of this practice. This is a good council practice to return to regularly. Describing the neuroscience around positive mind states can be very productive.

Things to Remember

Remember the diversity of your students. Some may not have parents, so you would not use parents as an example of what you would be grateful for. Find basic examples like being grateful for breath, water to drink, and for the sunshine.

Interconnection Lessons

Once we have generated positive qualities through inner practice, we can learn to offer them into the world. Mindfulness Without Borders, for example, is a remarkable organization that travels around the world leading what they call the Mindfulness Ambassador Council. They train students in mindfulness of the body, heart, and mind, and then go further by training students to go back into their communities to offer mindful service projects. They have taught in Rwanda, Kenya, Israel, and many other countries where these types of projects are so needed.

Even without telling kids to bring mindfulness into the world, I hear amazing stories of students teaching their friends and families. A parent once told me that she was hosting her daughter's birthday party, and there was a lot of chaos upstairs where all the 10-year-olds were playing. There was quite a ruckus, and then all of a sudden everything was quiet. The parents all looked at each other, and one ran upstairs to see all the kids silently practicing mindfulness.

Later the daughter came down and told her mother that two kids had gotten in a fight over a toy, and they all decided together to stop and take some mindful breaths. The student had only been in my class for a few weeks, but she was already becoming a mindfulness ambassador. Without being told, students begin paying it forward.

Students have told me that when they heard gunshots outside of their windows, they taught their little siblings breathing and relaxation exercises. I even had a 13-year-old therapy client who told me that he had been learning to observe when his mom got angry and send her caring thoughts instead of reacting. This was to the initial consternation and eventual deep appreciation of the mother.

We can teach games and practices to help kids integrate mindfulness into their lives. We can create service projects, school-wide discussions, and online mindful community boards with students around the world. Our mindfulness and heartfulness practices can evoke within us and our communities values of compassion and integrity. Once we have cultivated these virtues, we can learn how to communicate them with others and live in a sustainable way. In a very real way, our world depends on it.

Mindful Communication

Mindful listening is when we let go of our agendas and ideas to truly hear another person's perspective. We often have very firm impressions of the people we like and the people we don't like. Learning to see through our judgments can be hard work, but it allows us to be more friendly and positive. Being a good friend, teammate, or member of any group is determined by how well we can listen and be present with others. We can only really understand what someone is saying if our mind is clear from distractions and judgments.

The other part of mindful communication is mindful speaking, or speaking authentically. Instead of saying what we think others want to hear, we can learn to speak our inner truth. This means using our mindfulness to be aware of what is going on inside, and then being brave enough to share this with others. When you can really speak your truth and truly listen, that is when true friendship and connection occurs.

Learning Objectives

- Cultivating empathic and attentive listening skills.
- Building communication and friendship skills.
- Learning to speak from the heart and build authenticity.

Preparation

This exercise works best in a circle. Use a talking piece to pass around so that each student can have a chance to share. If you break students into pairs, it's important that each pair is not too close to another.

Sample Script: Present Moment Conversation

In our lesson today, we will learn to communicate from the present moment instead of simply sharing past experiences or ideas about the future. Making a present moment statement means simply stating what you experience right now in your body. You can say what sensations you feel in your body, what you see, hear, smell, or taste. You can also share your emotions, like if you are nervous, happy, or excited.

An example would be, "In the present moment I am aware of the sound of cars going by." Or, "In the present moment I am aware of feeling nervous." You will say this short statement and remember not to go into details about it. After you say you hear the cars going by you wouldn't say, "and that reminds me of something my sister said to me while we were driving in the car this morning." You are simply stating the present moment experience. We are learning to share and listen in the present moment about what is really going in our bodies and hearts."

Let's begin by getting our mindful bodies on and

looking inside to see all the experiences happening in our bodies.

For one minute, open up your listening ears to every sound near and far. Now for one minute feel all the sensations throughout your whole body. Now for another minute check in to see what emotions are in your body.

We can sit for one more minute and open our awareness as big as the sky. You can notice sensations, emotions, sounds, or whatever is happening in the present moment. If you notice thoughts, you can watch them float by like clouds in the sky.

Now we are going to keep our eyes closed and continue to practice our mindfulness, and as we do this we are going to learn how to speak mindfully. We will go around in a circle. When it is your turn you can look inside and say what you are experiencing in the present moment. Start your sentence with "In the present moment I am aware of . . ." Some examples would be: "In the present moment I am aware of an itch on my hand." "In the present moment I am aware of feeling nervous." If you notice you are thinking a lot, you can say, "In the present moment I am aware of my busy mind."

We can go around in a circle a few times and everyone can share what they are experiencing in the present moment. Remember to keep your eyes closed and focus inside. Don't try to come up with what you are going to say before your turn. See if you can simply listen when you are not speaking, and when it is your turn say whatever is true in the moment.

With older students, you can continue the session in dyads (pairs). Ask the students to shift their chairs so that they are sitting with a partner.

Sit in a comfortable position with your back straight and your body relaxed. Let your eyes close and focus inside. Take a slow, deep breath and allow the breath to be just as it is. When you are ready, open your eyes softly but keep your body mindful. One student at a time will share a few words about his or her mindful experience with the statement, "In the present moment I am aware of . . ." After a mindful statement has been made, each student can take a mindful breath and then the other student shares a mindful statement.

Remember not to go into stories or explanations. Stay in the present.

If you feel nervous or uncomfortable, you can always share that, saying, "In the present moment I am aware of feeling nervous."

After a few minutes, have the students close their eyes and take some mindful anchor breaths and notice what they feel like inside. Then let the students thank each other and orient themselves back to the room.

Dialogue

This is a very different way of communicating than how we usually talk. I like to ask students, "What would it be like if we always talked like this to each other?"

This is also a great time to have a dialogue about insecurity. You can ask students to share if they ever feel nervous or uncomfortable when they are talking with friends or family. You can ask kids if they ever feel judged or like they have to put on an act.

You can also use a teaching story or a quote and invite kids to share.

Be yourself, everyone else is taken.

—Oscar Wilde

Love is the only force capable of transforming an enemy into a friend.

—Martin Luther King Jr.

You cannot shake hands with a clenched fist.

—Indira Gandhi

Journaling Prompts

- Drawing: Draw a picture of the whole class sharing mindful words.
- Writing: How was that different than the usual way you talk with people?
- What did you notice in yourself as you were talking and listening?
- What would the world be like if this was the way everyone talked to each other?

World Discovery

"Notice the way you usually talk to people and see if you can bring in more present moment statements. You don't need to only speak present moment statements, but see if you can learn to be more authentic and tell people what is really going on inside. You can also work on your mindful listening skills. When someone is talking to you, see if you can really listen instead of just waiting for your turn to talk. See of you can suspend judgment about that person. After all, most of our judgments are based on experiences or learning from the past, not what we are experiencing right now."

Age and Stage

K–5 students can learn how to speak from the present moment but sometimes need more explanation of the parameters. It can be helpful to begin by having them share what they see, what they smell, and what they feel and going through all the senses so they understand what present moment senses are. This can be a wonderful exercise to practice several times a day, inviting students into the present moment when they come into school, after transitions, or whenever there is a disturbance in the room.

Sixth–12th-grade students can really absorb these lessons to gain new perspectives on how they communicate with family, friends, and teachers. If there's time, the practice can be begin in a circle and then continue in dyads where students can practice speaking to one another from the present moment.

Many adolescents are grappling with conflict arising from a deep desire to be authentic and real and a simultaneous deep desire to fit in. This practice can be especially meaningful, as it suggests to students that they can be accepted exactly as they are and not need to put on any masks.

Things to Remember

Speaking authentically can be an edgy experience for students. It can bring up a lot of insecurity, especially when youth speak to each other one on one. This practice should never be required for a student who is not comfortable with it.

The role of the teacher is to compassionately remind students whenever they begin to stray into thoughts rather than stay with present moment experiences. It takes a while for students to learn how to communicate from direct experience; it takes teachers time to learn this art, too. Remember your own practice to teach this well.

Natural World Lesson

The natural world has a lot to teach us about mindfulness. If you have access to nature trails or a garden, it can be wonderful to bring students to a natural space and give them time to sit and listen to the sounds, smell the smells (both good and bad), feel the caress of the breeze, and see the beautiful colors. No need to turn this into a complex practice; being with trees and birds has the natural capacity to help all of us relax and get back in touch with our bodies. You can tell kids the importance of finding a "sit spot" at home where they can chill out and connect with nature.

We can also learn to get in touch with the elements of nature within our own bodies. Even if there are no trees or animals around, we can explore nature in our own consciousness. Earth, fire, water, air, and space all have corresponding feelings in our bodies. A natural word practice helps kids feel into their solidity, creativity, calmness, flow, and spaciousness.

Learning Objectives

- Cultivating a sense of connectedness and stability.
- Connecting to the natural world.
- Heightening the senses and attuning to the body.

Preparation

It is ideal to do this practice outdoors, but if that's not possible you can do it inside. You could have pictures of the classical elements, or actually bring in water and earth to give children visual and visceral images. It is great to point out the classical elements that surround us: the sun as fire, ocean as water, ground as earth, breeze as air, and the space that permeates all things.

Sample Script: Mindful Elements

One of the best ways to practice mindfulness is to be mindful in nature. The natural world has many teachings for us. If we want to understand stillness, watching a tree can teach us a lot. If we want to understand how to focus, we can watch a hawk flying. When we are disconnected from nature, we may forget that we are part of the web of life. If we become mindful about nature, we will not litter or do something harmful to the Earth. On the contrary, if we mindfully feel how we are part of the Earth, we will want to take care of it.

We can also learn a lot from the classical elements of nature. Earth, fire, water, and air are four elements we see in the world, but we also can feel them in our bodies. For our mindfulness lesson, we will become aware of what these four sensations feel like within the body as well as becoming aware of the fifth element of space.

You can sit tall and proud while letting your body be relaxed. Let your eyes close or gaze downward. Use your anchor breath, noticing every in breath and out breath.

Bring to mind the image of a mountain and feel as if you were strong and solid, like a mountain. With every breath, you can feel more and more solid on the Earth, feeling the earth elements in your body.

Bring to mind the image of a still lake and feel as if you were calm and flowing like a lake. With every breath, imagine yourself calm and serene like the water element.

Bring to mind an image of the sun and feel as if your body was shining in all directions. With every breath, feel as if your body is shining like the element of fire.

Bring to mind the image of leaves shaking in the wind and notice all the different sensations moving around your body. With each breath, notice the constantly shifting sensations of the wind element.

Finally, imagine you were floating in outer space and get the feeling that there was nothing around you, totally spacious. With every breath, feel as if you were floating and feel the element of space.

Now become aware of the room around you and feel yourself sitting on the ground. When you are ready slowly, open your eyes and let's share with each other what we learned.

Journaling Prompts

- Drawing: Draw the way your body felt in each element.
- Writing: What did you notice when you were feeling these elements?

- What was your favorite element you felt in your body, and why?
- Were some elements easier or harder to feel?

World Discovery

"Find a quiet place in nature, or even next to a plant, and sit silently. Really open your senses to what the natural world has to say. Allow yourself to be *interested* in what nature has to say to you. This is your 'sit spot,' and you can go to this place whenever you want to relax and be mindful. You can go there every day, even if it's just for a minute, and listen to nature."

Age and Stage

Young children love to do this elemental practice. It is helpful to use visuals and have them really imagining they are a mountain. You can have young students picturing themselves as all types of animals and natural elements, seeing how this makes them feel. Imagining they are little mice often makes them feel safe, whereas imagining they are lions makes them feel strong.

Field trips in nature also make wonderful outings. Kids love to make lists of things to identify or find different kinds of flowers or trees, different colors, or different sounds—and check the things off their list as they find them. Engaging students with the natural world is interactive rather than a one-directional textbook or computer-based learning. Much can be learned from nature as an interactive teacher.

Things to Remember

Students sometimes feel uncomfortable in nature. Be sensitive to the fact that some children have had little contact with the natural world and may be afraid of germs and dirt.

Of course bringing children into nature has its own precautions. Allergies, bees, pollen, and other concerns need to be dealt with. You need to know your students and their parents in terms of what they are comfortable with.

Practicing Distraction

With this practice students get a clear understanding of how their minds wander even though they are trying to keep a sharp focus. Once students are able to reflect on their own attention, emotions, and bodies (as they have learned to do in previous lessons), we can begin to play with the ways the mind gets carried away. This game is especially helpful when students are distracted, for example, by their friends or sounds outside the room, and you can show them what it is like to work with it. It is one thing to be able to be mindful when everything is quiet, but this practice helps us be mindful amid the chaos of everyday life.

Learning Objectives

- Attention skills to hone a child's capacity to work with distractions.
- Strengthening impulse control with the capacity to not become distracted.
- Working with distractions collectively benefits the classroom environment.

Preparation

During the class you will be making noises and will need to have space to walk around. In many classrooms there are boxes of pencils, books, and other objects you can use to make noises. You can use whichever objects are around to rustle and shake. If you are in an empty room, you can bring some shakers, bells, or other noise-making tools.

Sample Script: The Distraction Game

Does anyone know what the word distraction *means? Now that we know how to sit with our mindful bodies and use our mindfulness to stay focused, do you think you can stay focused even if I try to distract you? Who wants to be my volunteer? Now you (the volunteer) are going to try to sit totally still, using your anchor breath to stay focused, and I'm going to try to distract you. See if you can stay totally still with your eyes closed even while I am making all these silly noises all over the place.*

Students are usually excited to play this game. As the student is sitting, you walk around shaking boxes of pencils and rustling papers. It's fine if the student opens his or her eyes, just voice a gentle reminder to go back to breath and focus. Once you finish and ask who else wants to try, frequently all the students are interested. You can have everyone get their mindful bodies on and practice their mindful breathing. This can lead to some very interesting conversations about distraction.

It can also be very beneficial to recruit a distractor's assistant. This can often be the student who is the most distracting student in the class. Make sure the student knows not to touch anyone or make noises that are too loud. It's wonderful to have enough time to play with distraction—perhaps over the course of several classes—so that each student feels what it is like to distract and be distracted. This empowers them to understand what distraction and impulsivity feels like inside and to be more empowered.

Dialogue

I frequently tell students, "It is often said that goldfish have terrible memories. The truth is that a goldfish has an attention span of nine seconds, while we only have an attention span of eight seconds. It looks like goldfish have a better attention span than we do. Let's all share stories of how we get distracted in our lives."

It can also be helpful to ask students what distraction feels like in their bodies. When students can feel the physical experience of distraction, it becomes easier for them to cultivate impulse control. It's great to use quotes for dialogue that students will find engaging, such as "The true mind can weather all lies and illusions without being lost. The true heart can touch the poison of hatred without being harmed" (this is a quote from the television show *Avatar: The Last Airbender*).

Another quote that could inspire conversation would be something like the following: "When I dance, I dance, when I sleep, I sleep; yes, and when I walk in a beautiful orchard, if my thoughts drift too far off matters for some part of the time, for some other part I led them back again to the walk, the orchard, the sweetness of this solitude, to myself" (Michel de Montaigne).

Journaling Prompts

- Drawing: Draw a picture of what it would look like if nothing could distract you.
- Writing: What does it feel like in your body when you are distracted?
- How would building your attention help you in your life?
- What are some ways in which you distract others?

World Work

Tell the students that they can use the distraction game in their lives as an opportunity to come back to their attention. You might suggest that they can set moments in the day, such as when a bell rings at school or a phone rings, to take three mindful breaths. Remind them that every time they hear a loud noise or someone walks in the room, they have an opportunity to notice the distraction and return to their anchor breath. This doesn't mean that they ignore the sound, just that they don't get lost in thoughts about it. Remind students that they can practice wherever they are. Especially when reading, practicing the piano, or doing anything else that takes focus, encourage them to see how distractions affect them and use distractions as practices to strengthen their "attention muscles."

Age and Stage

K–5 students usually love playing this game. The session can last from 15 to 20 minutes. There are many variations of the game, and it can be used again and again. When a child or the whole class seem particularly distracted, you can ask if they want to play the distraction game.

Sixth–12th-grade students can take the basic premise of this game and go further. This can be a full 30-minute or hour-long class with the practice and discussion around distraction. As the students are focusing, you can say words or tell a story and try to get them to see if they can keep their attention on their breath rather than getting lost in the story. You can get different students to say funny things and have the students practice maintaining their anchor breath. This becomes a great way to practice together.

Things to Remember

This is a more advanced practice, so you'll want to be sure that your students have developed some level of comfort and skill with their awareness of the body, the anchor breath, and awareness of thoughts.

When doing the distraction game, it is important to remember that certain students have nervous systems that are more sensitive than others. When you're making noises or walking around while students have their eyes closed, some class members may feel fear or even trauma. Make sure to make noises not too loud or abrupt, and keep an especially watchful eye on the class.

If you invite a student to help in you creating distraction, make clear to the helper that they shouldn't get too close to any students or make too loud a noise.

Mindful Engagement

This final lesson is aimed at helping students integrate their mindfulness practice into their daily lives. To do this it is very helpful for students to begin teaching these practices to each other. We also explore how students can come up with a way to bring mindfulness into the world. Students can become ambassadors of mindfulness. They can bring their compassion, attention, and embodiment into the world as an empowering gift for others.

Learning Objectives

- Integrating the mindfulness, heartfulness, and embodiment practices into daily life.
- Building the sense of confidence and empowerment that comes from teaching to others.
- Building an empathic community.

Preparation

Students will spend time in groups and will need their mindfulness journals for this exercise.

Sample Script

We can learn to be mindful in all aspects of our lives. We can be mindful when we are brushing our teeth, walking down the street, or talking with a friend. The only difference between mindfully walking and mindlessly walking is that when you walk mindfully, you know you're walking. Usually, when we walk down the street, we are thinking about a million things in the past and future, and we miss all of the amazing sounds, smells, and sights of the moment. When you are mindfully eating, you know you are eating and you get to taste everything better. Remember that raisin? Remember how amazing it tasted and felt? When you are mindfully brushing your teeth, you know you are brushing your teeth and you can enjoy it, as well as being more focused and cleaning every tooth.

In this lesson we will learn how to bring mindfulness into our everyday lives. Mindfulness is not just a practice to use when we are sitting down with our eyes closed. When you bring your mindfulness into the world, you cannot help but be more aware and empathic. In this lesson we will actually decide ways that we can bring what we have learned in all of our lessons into the world.

Let's all get our mindful bodies on and practice some anchor breaths.

When you are ready, you can continue being mindful and bring into your mind a moment when someone was really kind to you. Maybe this was a teacher, a friend, or someone else who gave you a gift, said a nice thing, or just gave you a hug. Keep picturing this moment as if you had a television in your mind and you were watching it on the screen. How does your body feel when you are picturing this kindness?

Now that you have this kind feeling in your heart, let's imagine a kind act that you could do for someone else. Maybe you picture saying something nice to a friend, picking a flower and giving it to your teacher, or any other kind act. Picture doing this in your mind, as if you were watching an inner TV screen, and see how this feels in your body.

Now we can make a commitment within ourselves to bring our heartfulness into the world. Let's feel inside of ourselves all that we have learned from mindfulness, embodiment, and heartfulness and imagine bringing all these strengths to the world.

Dialogue

In the dialogue students can spend time sharing with each other a kind act we can commit to. Older students or a whole class can even come up with mindful service projects together. This is a time to talk about how to bring mindfulness into the world.

There are many wonderful quotes and stories to help inspire this discussion.

Don't ask what the world needs. Ask what makes you come alive, and go do it. Because what the world needs is people who have come alive.

—Howard Thurman

You have brains in your head. You have feet in your
shoes. You can steer yourself any direction you choose.
—Dr. Seuss, *Oh! The Places You'll Go*

Journaling Prompts

- Drawing: Draw a picture of you giving your act of kindness.
- Writing: What is your vision of how you can bring your heartfulness into the world?
- How could you teach other people mindfulness?
- What qualities have you developed that you can offer to the world?

World Discovery

Having students choose a mindfulness service project will serve the student and the community. Let them take some time understand which qualities they have cultivated inwardly that they want to share with the world. Some examples would be going to younger classes and teaching gratitude lessons or committing to being nicer to their siblings. The mindful service work can be simple commitments of how they want to change in the world or real projects that they can do themselves or in a larger group.

Age and Stage

K–5 students can visualize themselves being mindful in the world and then writing about this. It's a good game to play and strengthens their ability to respond in the future in ways they have already imagined.

Sixth–12th-grade students can visualize how they want to be in future situations and explore the subtleties of their emotional responses and what holds them back from being their full selves. Students can plan ways to be mindful in their lives, and the whole class can come up with a mindfulness project.

Things to Remember

It is important to be cognizant of cultural diversity issues. Each student has different resources and obstacles. When inviting students to create their mindfulness projects, make sure you are sensitive to each child's world.

Integration

❋

We have made our way through the inner valley of personal practice and up to the peaks of witnessing how these teachings can work wonders, small and large, for our students. We can now begin to more fully, deeply, and consciously integrate our inner learning with our outer world.

We learn by stumbling, dusting ourselves off, courageously trying again, and keeping our hearts open through all the inevitable bumps and turns in the road. As my psychology mentor, Michael Kahn, used to say, "We all get into trouble. It's how we get out of trouble that's important." In this final chapter, we explore how to roll with the inevitable difficulties, celebrate our successes, and get the support we need.

Our solo mindfulness practice extends into a world where it is always tested. When you're learning how to kayak, you're taught in a calm part of the river so you can get your bearings. The calm practice is indispensable, but the expertise is developed in the swirls and crash of the flowing river. In the same way, sitting silently for mindfulness is the placid training ground for the social and emotional swirl of the world we live in. The goal of mindfulness is not to make everything placid and emotionally flat, it's to learn how to flow through the world as it is. A young woman in a high-school class summed this up well in a discussion after we had been silently witnessing our inner emotional waves. She said, "I guess if there were no waves, then we wouldn't be able to go surfing." Instead of teaching us to retreat from life, mindfulness gives us the strength to dive in. It gives us the emotional resilience to fall in love with our world without trying to change it, to love our lives as they are.

Whichever group of youth you teach, you will inevitably meet resistance, from them and from your own inner saboteur. This is not a mistake or even a problem. Resistance is our greatest teacher. Your family may not understand what you are doing, your colleagues and administrators may be skeptical, and your students may roll their eyes or make fart noises during the silent practices. Don't worry; this is all part of the process. Stay connected to your intention, your heart, and your body.

Sometimes in a silent practice a child will start laughing. Pretty soon the whole room will explode in giggles. I usually let the class laugh as long as they need to, but I tell them to notice the feelings in their bodies as they do it. Mindful laughing exercises are fun. Afterward I ask the students what it was like to be aware of their laughter. The exploration of how laughter feels and the awareness of distraction is a great awareness game. What seems like an obstacle is almost always the most important lesson. If there is a resistance in the field, then there is some fear, some insecurity, some way in which students don't feel comfortable with what is happening. Meeting resistance with interest and compassion invites honest communication, which transforms into understanding and connection.

For an example of how to meet resistance with interest we can look at two classrooms I worked with in Vermont. In one high school I spent the day jumping from classroom to classroom, teaching and learning with the students. I made a special note of two classrooms across the hall from each other. One was the honors class. When I entered they all sat up tall and respectfully said hello. When I asked if they had heard of mindfulness they all raised their hands and shared clear answers of what they remembered from previous classes. They said that mindfulness made them calm, happy, and less angry. They were very respectful, but I did have some questions about how honest they were being. I thought, "Is this their real experience or are they just wanting to share the 'right' answer?"

As I crossed the hall my guide told me that next was the low-achieving class. As I entered I saw a very different sight. The students were slouched over their desks. The boys had hoodies over their heads, and the girls wore dark eye makeup. When I asked if they had heard about mindfulness, one girl huffed and said, "I can't do mindfulness, I have ADHD." Now *that* was an honest answer. "What do you mean you can't do it? What happens when you try?" I was genuinely interested.

"Well my mind just goes all over the place and I try to focus on my breath but it doesn't work," she replied. As I asked her questions about this, the others chimed in and all of them seemed to dislike mindfulness because when they tried it their minds were all over the place and it seemed impossible. There was a general sense of low self-esteem and hopelessness in the room. So I asked them what they thought ADHD was and we had a long and engaging conversation about distraction, social insecurity, emotional reactivity, and inner critical voices. I could see how these teens had built belief systems around their own inadequacies. It felt like I was wrestling with them to let go of these limiting beliefs so they could get a glimpse of their own inner wisdom.

"You're all saying how annoyed you are that your minds are

so wild," I said. "That's why I love mindfulness. My mind is all over the place, so I practice mindfulness and instead of being tossed around by my thoughts and feelings I am able to balance them." The class was engaged at this point, and we did a few mindfulness practices around witnessing thoughts and difficult emotions. Their teacher told me the next day that he had never seen his class so interested and that all they wanted to talk about since then was how their minds worked, what ADHD was, and how mindfulness could help.

It's wonderful when I walk into a class and they're well behaved, but resistance has its own special teaching. When resistance is present, there is something very honest being spoken. If there is resistance, there is a good chance you are moving faster than the students can follow, are not engaging them, or are speaking a way they can't understand. You have probably gone outside of their range or the metaphorical bus has left and someone has been left behind. Resistance tells us that the teacher–student relationship has been broken. Instead of trying to push our lesson we need to tend to the relationships. This is the teacher's opportunity to learn about his or her students. We need to turn the bus around and make sure we have not left until every one is on board.

If we don't turn the bus around, and instead keep running away from resistance, we perpetuate a cycle in which we resist resistance. The result of this is usually that the tension becomes even more uncomfortable and we resist even more, becoming more disconnected from our students and ourselves. When we are in this cycle, as our own stress builds, we get frustrated with our students and project onto them. When we don't bring our kind awareness to this situation, our students get spun into the stress cycle. When our students are stressed they act out and resist, which causes even more stress for us. And so on and so on . . .

The good news is that this stress chain can be broken at any time. The moment you notice resistance, from the inside or outside, is an opportunity to turn your ship of awareness directly into the storm. Instead of resisting resistance, we can bring compassion to whatever difficult experience we are having in our minds, bodies, and hearts. As we relax our nervous systems and open our hearts, we'll develop an empathic presence, and our students will be the benefactors. Our own inner turning pulls students into the same conscious current. Of course, once our class is more calm and collected, we will have fewer external stressors to deal with. Instead of the backward stress cycle, we can create a positive feedback loop with our practice. We can turn the wheel toward stress or compassion. The choice is ours.

Personal Practice

It has been repeated many times in this book, and I repeat it again here: *mindfulness begins with our own practice.* Let your practice sustain you. Let it be your refuge and your ally.

Finding a space within your house and scheduling time is usually necessary to really commit yourself to an ongoing practice. Even if all you do is spend 20 minutes every morning sitting still and not being carried off by the million tasks and technologies that clamor for your attention, this will be of greatest benefit to you. You'll be reinforcing an inner voice that says, "I am committed to an authentic connection to my body, mind, and heart."

You are not alone on this path. Even if you live in a community where no one else is interested in mindfulness, there is a great movement under way of which you are a part. Use the remarkable wealth of talks and classes on mindfulness that are free online. Of course, if there's a center that teaches mindfulness nearby, or a sitting group, these are among the best ways to support your practice. If you can organize a practice group in your school you can weave this practice ever more into your daily life. There's something about coming together that inspires practice. Knowing that you are not alone and that there is a community of people doing the same practice is an amazing support.

Find my place and time for sitting and breathing

Finding a teacher is also of great help. You don't need to find some enlightened guru; someone who's a little further down the path than you are will do. When you reach certain states of awareness, or when fears begin arising, it's indispensable to have a teacher who has been where you are and with whom you can talk things through. It can also be wonderful to have a therapist with whom you can discuss your journey and discoveries. Psychology doesn't need to be limited to fixing problems; a great therapist can be like a research assistant who guides you through an inner exploration and helps you connect with who you truly are.

As you walk the mindful path, remember to take it easy. We aren't trying to *get* somewhere with mindfulness. We are simply learning to be fully present with what is. Bringing mindfulness to eating peaches, listening to our favorite music, and cleaning the floor is an art. As we do the laundry, we can get so attuned that folding pants becomes a dance and listening to a friend becomes a mindful exploration into emotion and connection. This is where we take our mindfulness lessons from kids. Let yourself be awe-inspired and exhilarated by every seemingly ordinary moment. Let your body play. Let your mind be free. Let your heart be open. Let yourself feel the interconnected web of which you are an integral part.

Integration Exercises

In bringing mindfulness into your work, you can begin by gaining a clear vision of what you have to offer and what is needed. Spend some time on the following three exercises to be mindful of each answer. Finding your path in the world mirrors your own self-discovery. As you get to know your passions and your gifts, you can learn to link them up with what is needed in the world. Your authentic path is never based on doing what others think you should do. Your most profound offering is the one that arises from getting ever closer to who you truly are. Only that can make you happy and give you that sense of offering something meaningful.

Exercise: Day 1

What are your passions, personal strengths, and life tools? Take an hour to meditate on the three questions that follow to figure out what you have to offer those you are working with. Write out your answers to these questions and make sure to wait a day before doing the second exercise.

- Passions: What is your passion? What makes you feel alive? What work would you do if you won the lottery, not for money or prestige, but if you were doing it just for the love of the experience?

- Personal Strengths: What inner traits—like compassion, intelligence, or willpower—naturally arise within you? Maybe you are physically strong or coordinated. Maybe you are a natural leader or have good decision-making skills. What are the qualities of your personality that shine forth and that other people reflect about you?
- Life Tools: What external skills and tools do you have to offer? Do you have a particular degree, a certification, or life experience? Do you have a special connection with a local school or access to other resources?

Exercise: Day 2

Look to the communities you are part of and spend an hour figuring out what they genuinely need. Without judging, you can simply see how certain attributes are not developed or resources are lacking. Examples would be seeing a lack of fresh food and clean air in particular areas or regions or observing that a particular group lacked access to a certain type of learning. You may see a lack of emotional intelligence or impulse control in certain friends or colleagues. Without judgment, see what basic needs are not being met. Write down your answers and wait a day before the next exercise.

- Family: Ask yourself what it is your family and loved ones need. How are the people directly around you struggling or in need of wellness? What emotional, physical, and external needs are there?

- Friends and Colleagues: Look at the different worlds you walk in and take an eagle-eye view at what needs there are. If you are in a school or service center, try to get an objective view of what inner and outer resources are needed.
- Community: Look at the community and society around you. Look at the town or city you live in and see the diverse groups. What inner and outer resources are missing from these communities?

Exercise: Day 3 (and Beyond!)

It's now time to integrate, to look at what we've discovered in the first two exercises and piece the information together. What links can you make between the resources you have and the needs of your world? Make a map of all your resources and all the needs of your world and draw some connecting lines. See what links feel most inspiring.

Let's say you see that the level of communication skills in your colleagues at work is very low and you have been trained in and have a lot of enthusiasm for nonviolent communication or mindful communication. This represents a natural and perfect link between a resource and a need, and you can begin to find the sweet spots of how you might want to work with this link. In exploring our genuine strengths and the needs in the world, we can learn to give our greatest offering.

Heartfulness Send Out

※

These teachings have been passed down from generation to generation, from loving parents to their children and from master teachers to their students. The teachings are very simple. Strive to open your heart, open your mind, and be fully present in your body. There is no religion to this; it doesn't even need to be called mindfulness. This is about kindness, insight, and taking responsibility for our lives. This is about falling in love with life exactly as it is.

The revolution of mindfulness in education is not some overthrow of the government or radical change of policy. We long to see everyone happy, to see everyone getting their basic human needs met. We want everyone to taste what it's like to be fully alive. We are not fighting anyone with this revolution. Everyone is invited, and no one is coerced. No one needs to use this manual or subscribe to any theory. We can learn to offer these teachings unconditionally, without assuming that we will get something in return, like a quieter class, for example.

As each reader carries these practices into their lives and work, the environment of our world is being affected. This is a revolution, a transformation from the inside out. This transformation isn't actually for us. We can step out of I, me, and mine consciousness and realize that all the inner and outer work we are doing is an offering to the world.

We have been gifted with our bodies, our breath, water to drink, and myriad wonders around us. As we practice mindfulness, we can reconnect to our ability to appreciate and feel connected to our lives. With this appreciation, may we learn how to be reverent and caring not just to each other but to our natural environment. The deeper the interconnection we feel the harder it is to be mean to someone, or to pollute our Earth. This is our Earth, this is our community, these are our kids who will grow to become the teachers and caretakers of tomorrow. May the work that we all have done here seed a future that is so intact and vibrant that books like this won't even need to be written. As foxes don't need to teach their young how to be a foxes, may we all one day be so intuitively mindful that our children never need to hide their true selves. May the authenticity of all children everywhere grow unobstructed. May our commitments toward compassion and wisdom stay strong, blossoming into a world of compassion, presence, and happiness. May it be.

CURRICULUM SAMPLES

There are many different styles of mindfulness-based curricula. I offer a variety of the best curricula to introduce you to the breadth of ways that mindfulness can be adapted into youth-based settings. Vinnie Ferraro was the training director for Challenge Day, then the Mind Body Awareness Project, and now Mindful Schools. Vinnie's style of teaching is vulnerable, hilarious, sometimes a little shocking, and always deeply authentic. He grew up hard, as he will be the first to tell you, with poignant self-disclosures of drugs and incarceration. From this gritty upbringing he helped the Mind Body Awareness Project develop a curriculum for incarcerated youth that is just raw enough to engage those who may otherwise pass these teachings off as weak or cheesy.

Meanwhile Chris Cullen and Richard Burnett, two British schoolteachers, have created the Mindfulness in Schools Project. In creating their .b curriculum, they asked themselves how to make mindfulness accessible to kids who are constantly texting and bored by the idea of sitting in silence. Their answer is to use funny British humor, like the acronym FOFBOC, for Feet On Floor, Bum On Chair. They use amazing cartoons, videos, and other engaging material to help make mindfulness accessible to the students. This curriculum may not work for incarcerated youth, and the MBA Project curriculum may not work for British schoolchildren, but the authenticity and skill of each curriculum fulfills their goals beautifully.

The most beneficial teaching comes from a teacher's own authentic wisdom and is tailored to meet students exactly where they are. Of course training wheels are helpful when teaching a new subject, so in this section some samples of curricula are presented to give ideas of how these practices can be adapted. It can be helpful to look to a charismatic teacher for inspiration or a highly tuned curriculum like .b for ideas, but remember that the training wheels are only there to help you ride free.

There are many curricula that could have been chosen for this book, and here are presented five that represent various styles and serve different populations. Each sample lesson is accompanied by a brief description of the organization and how to follow up with them if you want further training. As education evolves in the digital age, some of these organizations have begun using online games, apps, and online community forums to meet students in their modern medium. Hopefully you will be heartened by what you see and inspired to create your own projects, drawing from your own expertise, and feeding your community exactly what it needs.

Mindful Schools

Mindful Schools is a nonprofit organization that offers professional training, in-class instruction, and other resources to support the integration of mindfulness in education. Their curriculum has been taught to more than 150,000 children and adolescents, and their professional trainings have reached thousands of educators, social workers, psychologists, parents, and other adults internationally. Learn more at www.mindful schools.org.

Mindful Schools Lessons on Thoughts

Key Points
This lesson is generally given after several weeks of practicing the basic mindfulness techniques such as mindful listening and mindful breathing.

When you use this lesson after students have become familiar with mindfulness, they will likely have noticed that when they try to be mindful of their breathing, their mind sometimes wanders away. Most likely, you have identified this with them over the past few weeks. Choose one of the lessons below based on what you think your classes are capable of. You may want to try the other lesson on another day.

Italics are instructions for you. Normal font is the script.

Past/Present/Future (best for 3rd–5th)
Raise your hand if when we do mindfulness you find mindful breathing easy. Raise your hand if you find it hard. Raise your hand if you notice that even though you are trying to stay focused on your breathing you often realize you are thinking about things instead.

When we can pay attention to our breath mindfully, we are in the present moment. But our mind has a habit of wandering to the past and the future to think about other things.

For example, let's say that where I am standing right now is the present, and I'm trying to pay attention to my breathing, but then my mind starts to think about lunch and wonder what I will be eating. *Move your body to the right.* My mind has gone into the . . . *let them answer*. Yes. And I notice that and then bring my mind back to my anchor, my breath.

And I am paying attention again . . . *pause a moment as you are paying attention* . . . and then my mind starts to remember what happened yesterday at recess. Oops, my mind has wandered into the . . . *move your body to the left and leave a pause to let them answer.* Yes, I have gone into the past. I notice that and then I bring my attention back to my breath, the . . . (*moving your body back to center*) *let them answer—present.*

Are you ready to try? Ok. We will be mindful of our breath for one minute and you will watch to notice if your mind escapes to the past or the future. We will start with both our hands resting on our belly. When you notice you are thinking about the future, take your right hand gently off your belly and over toward the right. *(Demonstrate)* When you notice you are thinking about the past, take your left hand gently off your belly and over toward the left. Then bring your attention back to your breathing.

Practice for 1–2 minutes

Raise your hand if you were able to just pay attention to your breath and no thoughts interfered.

Raise your hand if you noticed a thought.

Raise your hand if you noticed your mind wandering away to the past or the future.

Let them tell you where it went if they want.

Raise your hand if you had a thought about the past or the future, but you noticed it and you brought yourself back to the present.

See Wrap Up and Journal Questions below.

First Thought (best for K–2)

Raise your hand if sometimes you can focus on your breathing the whole time when we practice mindful breathing.

Raise your hand if sometimes your mind starts thinking and you forget about your breathing. Yes, sometimes our mind wanders away even when we ask it to stay put. For most of us this happens a lot. Today we are going to learn how to be mindful of our thoughts and return to our breathing.

Let's try one more minute of mindful breathing. Try to stay focused on every single breath. But raise your hand when the first thought pops up. It might be about something you've done, or something you are going to do, or what someone said. Whatever it is, just notice it, raise your hand, and then put your hand back on your breathing spot and continue breathing in and out. If another thought pops up in your mind, raise your hand again. We'll try this for every thought for one minute.

Practice one–two minutes.

Raise your hand if you were able to keep your attention on your breathing that whole minute. Raise your hand if your attention wandered away. Can anyone tell me what their first thought was?

Wrap Up

Everybody thinks. We can be mindful of thinking.

Sometimes we have thoughts we don't want to have. By noticing them we can more easily let go.

Sometimes we are thinking when we want to be listening to what someone is saying, so if we notice that, we can be mindful and come back to listening.

Sometimes, we have the same thoughts over and over, even though we don't need to. When we are mindful of them and we notice them, we don't believe them as much.

Now, you have a very useful mindful tool. For the next few days, try to notice your thoughts. You might notice them while you are in class, or on the playground, or at home.

Optional Journal/Drawing Questions
1. Draw a picture of what your mind looks like when it is thinking.
2. How many thoughts do you think a person has each day?
3. How do you feel when you are focused on your breathing? How do you feel when you are lost in thinking?

Close with bell & three mindful breaths.

Mindfulness Without Borders

Mindfulness Without Borders' educational programs aim to mitigate the constant state of stress and anxiety, high levels of information overload, and growing disconnection that our students and their educators experience. Through programs for both youth and the adults that surround them, we create an intimate and relational culture inside the classroom through results–driven instruction in skills that develop the whole student. With this framework, we help create school cultures that support and promote individuals to thrive—not just survive. The result is a change in mindset and lifestyle choices for high- and low-performing students, disadvantaged youth, and their more advantaged peers.

Since 2008, MWB has worked internationally with over 1,300 educators and 1,000 students in select locations in Rwanda, Nigeria, Uganda, Israel, Jamaica, Botswana, New Jersey, San Francisco, and Toronto. MWB's evidence-based Mindfulness Ambassador Council curriculum for high school youth contains 12 lessons that reinforce the social-emotional competencies and secular mindfulness practices students require to lead productive, responsible, and compassionate lives. A special eight-lesson interactive curriculum is available for individuals with alternative learning styles. See http://mindfulnesswithoutbor ders.org.

Mindfulness Ambassador Council: Handling Conflict Skillfully

Open the Council
Council members sit in a circle and start with a 3-minute practice breathing practice, called TUZA.

Note: *The facilitator explains that with a breathing practice, we can learn to calm our minds and find a place of stillness within ourselves. By just pausing and paying attention to our breath, we can calm our mind, body and heart even while the waves of emotion, thought and outside experiences wash over us. What we begin to discover is that we can't always control what happens to us in life, but we can control how we react.*

Here's How to TUZA:
- Sit in a comfortable position. Allow both soles of your feet to connect to the floor.
- Rest your hands on your thighs and let your shoulders drop.
- Gently close your eyes or look for a reference point somewhere on the floor where you can return your eyes when they get distracted and begin to wander around the room.
- Let your spine grow tall and noble like the trunk of a tall tree.
- Take a moment to notice how your body feels.
- Now, bring your attention to the flow of your breath.

- You don't need to breathe in a special way. Your body knows how to breathe.
- Simply notice each breath coming into the body with an inhale, and leaving the body with an exhale.
- If you notice your mind is caught up in thoughts, concerns, emotions or body sensations, know that this is normal.
- Notice what is distracting you and gently let it go by redirecting your attention back to the breath.
- Without thinking you can't do this, simply and as kindly as you can, turn to your attention back to breathing for another few moments.
- Allow each in-breath to be a new beginning and each out-breath a letting-go.
- When you are ready, slowly bring your attention back to the room.

Council Check-in
Share a word or image that comes to mind when you hear the word "conflict."

Council Guidelines
Note: The facilitator asks for six volunteers to take the talking piece and read the council guidelines out loud.
- Speak only when you have the talking piece
- Listen respectfully with an openness to multiple perspectives
- Speak from the heart and use "I" statements
- Say just enough
- What is said in the council stays in the council
- Do your best to attend all council meetings

Theme: Handling Conflict Skillfully
Conflict is about opposition—between individuals, groups or one's own thoughts and feelings. At its worst, two sides

are polarized into "us" versus "them." They have shut down communication and are unwilling to see any other perspective than their own. Whether we experience conflict at home, with friends, at work, within our communities, or even within our own minds, conflict makes most of us feel on edge, stressed or unsafe.

People respond to conflict in different ways—physically, emotionally and mentally. Some may feel an impulse to fight back, to run away, or to sweep the issue under the rug (fight, flight or freeze). Others may want to nurture self and others, and form alliances (tend and befriend). Suspending our auto-pilot reactions gives us the opportunity to consider whether anything else has triggered us and to choose a skillful response. Rather than react habitually, we can pause and explore constructive ways to deal with tensions and divisions. To resolve a conflict, it is important to differentiate between what we actually need and what we would like to get out of the situation. For example, do we want to win an argument? Or, do we just want the other person to hear our point of view?

It is helpful to check our own motivations, evaluate our thoughts clearly without being controlled by them, and deliberately think of others in choosing our response. We may experience anger, frustration, hurt or a mixture of feelings, but we are much more powerful than these emotions. We can choose to keep our needs and the other person's needs intact by asking, "What approach moves towards resolving the conflict, as opposed to furthering it? What can I do to navigate this situation without aggression and violence?" The mindful response in any given situation is to pause and notice our initial reaction and use this awareness to be more educated and responsible in the way we proceed. When we act with this type of discernment and restraint, we are more likely to handle conflict effectively.

Teaching Quote

"The ultimate measure of a man is not where he stands in a moment of comfort and convenience, but where he stands at times of challenge and controversy."
—Martin Luther King Jr., clergyman and activist

Council Dialogue

The participants pass the talking piece around the circle and answer the following questions:

- Tell a story about a time when you were in an argument with someone you completely disagreed with.
- Looking back from the other person's point of view, can you acknowledge their perspective?

Present Moment Tools

- Notice what thoughts and emotions you are experiencing before responding.
- Take a moment to place yourself in the other person's shoes.
- Speak your truth clearly, without aggression and violence.
- Use "I" statements and don't place blame.
- Brainstorm with those involved to negotiate alternative solutions.
- Seek counsel or mediation when additional advice is needed.
- Evaluate the short- and long-term consequences of your response.
- Maintain humility and explore ways to transform conflict into opportunity.
- Be courageous and act with compassion.

Mindfulness Practice: Loving-Kindness

The most important people in our lives are often not the ones who have the most knowledge or who are the most popular, but rather those who treat us and the world that surrounds them with empathy and compassion. The intent of this mindfulness practice is to experience what it feels like to allow a genuine sense of loving, empathetic concern for others to arise in our hearts. In this practice, we foster an attitude of love, compassion and a genuine wish for others to find happiness, knowing that the gift of wishing others happiness is also a present to ourselves.

Here's How:
- Sit in a comfortable position. Allow both soles of your feet to connect to the floor.
- Rest your hands on your thighs and allow your shoulders to drop.
- Close your eyes or soften your gaze downwards, look for a reference point somewhere on the floor that you can return your eyes to, when they get distracted and begin to wonder around the room.
- Allow your spine to grow tall and noble like the trunk of a tall tree.
- Focus your attention to the flow of your breath.
- Bring to mind someone dear to you, someone toward whom you feel deep gratitude and tenderness.
- As you hold this person in your thoughts, begin to send them well wishes for happiness, good health and peace.
- Now, begin to direct your well wishes to someone with whom you feel neutral—someone you neither like nor dislike. An example of this could be the bus driver, the corner storeowner or the waiter at a restaurant.
- As you hold this person in your thoughts, begin to send them well wishes for joy, health and peace with the same goodwill that you feel toward those who are close to you.
- If you get distracted, notice what distracted you and let it

go by redirecting yourself back to the practice of sending loving wishes.

- Now, bring to mind someone with whom you have been in disagreement. Send them well wishes too, knowing that just as you wish to be cared for, happy and peaceful, so do they.
- Now, extend your loving and kind wishes to everyone sitting in this council.
- Expand your wishes even further to include the students and teachers in your entire school, your neighborhood, your city, and then, to the whole world, knowing that as you wish to be loved and cared for, so do they.
- Bring you attention back to the flow of the breath and notice how you feel.
- When you feel ready, slowly open your eyes and bring your attention back to the circle.

Reflecting on the Practice
- How did it feel to offer care and kindness to a loved one?
- How did you feel in offering empathy to someone with whom you have difficulty?

Home Assignment
The facilitator reviews the home assignment and asks the council members to do their best to complete the assignment as it is an important part of the participant experience. As part of the council process, Mindfulness Ambassador Council members are encouraged to discover ways to bring more present moment awareness (mindfulness) into your daily life. In each home assignment, the mindfulness practice is referred to as **be.Mindful** *and the mindfulness activity is referred to as* **m.Activity.**
    b.Mindful: Take Time to TUZA for 3 minutes, twice a

day, to help bring your awareness back to your breath and stay in the present moment. Use the downloadable recording found in the podcast section on our website. http://mind fulnesswithoutborders.org/podcasts.

m.Activity: During the next week, **notice** when you are faced with a dilemma or you have a strongly held position about something. **Explore** what it may mean to respond with discernment and restraint in that situation. **Be aware** of what you feel in that moment. Bear in mind the short-and long-term consequences of your actions. **In your journal, summarize your findings** and address how you can act in a way that is consistent with your highest values.

Close the Council

Members stand in a circle to close the meeting with **Circle of Gratitude**. One person in the circle turns to the right and says to the person standing beside them, "Thank you for being here." Each message of thanks is passed from person to person, until everyone in the circle has said and received thanks.

The Mind Body Awareness Project

The Mind Body Awareness (MBA) Project is a California nonprofit dedicated to serving high-risk and incarcerated adolescents. Their mission is to help youth transform harmful behavior and live meaningful lives through the practice of mindfulness meditation and emotional awareness. MBA currently serves approximately 1,000 young people a year in juvenile halls, public high schools, and other community-based settings. Their highly skilled facilitators deliver an innovative and culturally relevant mindfulness-based curriculum via group and individual session formats in a language accessible to high-risk and incarcerated adolescents. The goal of their service is to provide comprehensive, continuity of care services to follow youths out of juvenile detention and into high schools to prevent future recidivism and violence-related behaviors. MBA's curriculum is gaining efficacy in the form of three peer-reviewed, scholarly journal articles suggesting its feasibility and preliminary effects on stress and self-regulation on high-risk and incarcerated youth. For more information and to join MBA's mailing list, go to www.mbaproject.org.

Two Sample Mindfulness Activities from the Mind Body Awareness Project

Activity 1: Still Chillen
Activity Type: Game
Materials Needed: Meditation Bell
"Still Chillen" is a game that we often employ when we first meet youth. It's a way to get the energy of the group flowing and can work as a great icebreaker when forming new groups, or a energy booster when the group energy is particularly low. The game points toward one aspect of mindfulness practice: That outside distractions can have the potential to make one react with unintentional behaviors. The goal is to get youth thinking (on an introductory level) how such distractions can sometimes influence their own behaviors, and that with practice, they can gain more autonomy over themselves.

Still Chillen Instructions
Have the youth (preferably 6–15 youth) sit in chairs in a circle. Explain to them that the object of "Still Chillen" is to

see who can last the longest without moving. Tell them that they can blink and breathe, but other than that if they moved they will be called out for that round. The idea is to not move until one youth is left not moving (that rounds winner). Let them stretch, laugh, and get any movement out prior to starting the 1st round. Then, count down from 5 and ring the meditation bell to start the activity. You may find that the youth erupt in laughter almost immediately. That's normal and you should facilitate the game two more times, each time encouraging them to try harder and to "breathe" to focus. After 3 rounds, lead a discussion with the following discussion questions:

• How did you stay still? What did you do with your mind? (Definitely ask the winners of each round).
• Did you notice a difference in each round?
• How did focusing on your breath help or not help?

Activity 2: Counting Rings Meditation
Activity Type: Meditation
Materials Needed: Meditation Bell
The "Counting Rings" Meditation is a great way for youth to become acquainted with their minds and can be employed in the group or one on one setting. MBA implements this activity in our second group module, usually in a group [of] 6–15 youth. The objectives of this activity is for youth to have an introductory experience of witnessing how their minds wander and how they have the potential to refocus their minds through the power of mental training.

Counting Rings Instructions
In a circle with 6–12 youth, explain to the group that you will be taking them through a meditation-based activity where they'll be learning more about the nature of their minds. Tell

them to attempt to count home many times you ring the meditation bell while everyone is meditating, and to be aware of how they keep count. The only rule is that they have to close their eyes, and they cannot count on their fingers (thus using the faculties of the mind). Pick a number and stay true to that number, then start the meditation with the first bell and ring the bell the amount of times you previously chose. Try not to ring the bell with the same amount of time in between rings (thus becoming predictable). Let your in-between time vary. After you've finished the activity (at MBA, we usually ring the bell about 12–15 times over the course of 5–7 minutes), close the meditation and process with the youth with the following discussion questions:

- How many times do you think I rung the bell?
- What did you do to keep your mind on the correct number of rings?
- Did you notice your mind wandering between the rings? If so, was it difficult to remember what ring we were on when I rung the bell?

The Mindfulness in Schools Project

Richard Burnett and Chris Cullen, co-founders of the Mindfulness in Schools Project, met in 2007. Along with Chris O'Neill, these schoolteachers had experienced the benefits of mindfulness themselves and wanted to bring it to life in the classroom. The .b curriculum is their flagship 9-week course that offers a way in to mindfulness that students find fun, accessible and of genuine use in their lives.

Today the course has been expanded as an offering for teachers, staff, and parents, as well as for primary students. It is being taught in 12 countries and translated into Spanish, Icelandic, Dutch, Danish, Finnish, German, French, and American English. Because .b is designed by teachers, it is packaged with a specific pedagogy that makes teaching—and learning—mindfulness approachable and relevant to school life, whether that be a stressed teen facing exams, a bullying issue on the playground, a performance moment in sports or music, or enhanced listening and interpersonal communications for teachers.

The audiovisual resources, animations, teacher lesson plans, student booklets, and rigorous certification program ensure authentic, current materials that are evidence-based and continually evolving. See pages 292 and 293 for a sample lesson from .b.

LESSON EIGHT .b

Pulling It All Together

☑ What have you found most useful?

☑ In what ways could one or two of these skills help change your life for the better?

☑ What advice would you give yourself to make the most of what you have learned?

(1) Direct Attention

Lesson One
Playing Attention
Training the muscle of your mind

Skills:
- Directing your attention
- Exploring and investigating what you find

Practices
- **'Aiming and sustaining'** attention on breathing for 2 mins
- Counting the number of **breaths in a minute**

(2) Accept and calm

Lesson Two
Turning Towards Calm

Skills:
- Calming the mind by 'anchoring' it in the body
- Relaxing and breathing with experiences, even difficult ones

Practices
- **FOFBOC:** A body scan with Feet on Floor, Bum on Chair
- Anchoring your mind in the sensations of the body

(3) Deal with worry

Lesson Three
Recognising Worry
Noticing how your mind plays tricks on you

Skills:
- Recognising what our minds do that makes us worry: we *interpret*, we *ruminate*, we *catastrophise*
- 'Un-worrying' via a 7/11
- Using *Beditation* to help us sleep

Practices
- **7-11**
- **Beditation** (lying down body scan)

LESSON EIGHT

.b

Pulling It All Together

4 Be here now

Skills:
* Stepping out of 'auto-pilot' mode
* Savouring the pleasant
* Responding rather than reacting

Practices
* .b
* Mindful **mouthful**
* Sitting like a statue for **15 minutes**

5 Move mindfully

Skills:
* Moving mindfully
* Bringing mindfulness to daily activity
* Aspiring to 'flow' or be 'in the zone'

Practices
* Mindful **walking**
* Mindful toothbrushing, **showering**, eating etc.

6 Step back

Skills:
* Seeing thoughts as traffic that flows through the mind
* Identifying 'thought-buses' that pass through your mind
* Recognising that you don't have to 'get on the bus' of difficult thoughts

Practices
* Observing thought-traffic
* Practising staying at the bus stop, rather than getting carried away

7 Befriend the difficult

Skills:
* Understanding stress
* Recognising your stress signature
* *Responding* to stress and difficult emotions rather than *reacting* to them

Practices
* Breathing with stress / letting it be

20

RESOURCES

For more resources from Daniel Rechtschaffen visit online at
www.mindfuleducation.com
www.danielrechtschaffen.com

Curriculum and Programs

- CARE for Teachers. http://www.care4teachers.org/
- CASEL: Collaborative for Academic, Social and Emotional Learning. http://casel.org/
- Center for Contemplative Mind in Society. http://www.contemplativemind.org/
- Holistic Life Foundation. http://www.hlfinc.org/services.htm
- Inner Kids Program. http://www.susankaisergreenland.com/inner-kids.html
- Hawn Foundation, MindUP Program. http://www.thehawnfoundation.org/mindup/
- Inner Resilience Program. http://www.innerresilience-tidescenter.org/
- Inward Bound Mindfulness Education. http://ibme.info/
- Lineage Project. http://www.lineageproject.org/
- Mind Body Awareness Project. http://www.mbaproject.org/

- Mindfulness-Based Cognitive Therapy (MBCT). http://www.mbct.com/
- Mindfulness in Schools Project. http://mindfulnessin schools.org/
- Mindfulness Without Borders. http://mindfulnesswithout borders.org/
- Mindful Schools, Program and Teacher Training. http://www.mindfulschools.org/
- PATHS Curriculum. http://www.prevention.psu.edu/proj ects/paths.html
- Still Quiet Place. http://www.stillquietplace.com/

Mindfulness Research and Institutions

- The Center for Compassion and Altruism Research and Education (Stanford). http://ccare.stanford.edu/
- The Center for Mindfulness in Medicine, Health Care, and Society. http://www.umassmed.edu/content.aspx?id=41252
- Greater Good (UC Berkeley). http://greatergood.berke ley.edu/
- Mind and Life Institute. http://www.mindandlife.org/
- Mindful Awareness Research Center (UCLA Semel Institute). http://marc.ucla.edu/
- Mindfulness in Schools Project, Research Summary. http://www.enhancementthemes.ac.uk/docs/documents/ impact-of-mindfulness—-katherine-weare.pdf
- Mindfulness Research Guide. http://www.mindfulexperi ence.org/

REFERENCES

Baer, R. A. (2003). Mindfulness training as a clinical intervention: A conceptual and empirical review. *Clin Psychol Sci Prac 10*(2), 125–43.

Biegel, G. M., Warren Brown, K., Shapiro, S. L., & Schubert, C. M. (2009). Mindfulness-based stress reduction for the treatment of adolescent psychiatric outpatients: A randomized clinical trial. *Journal of Consulting and Clinical Psychology, 77*(5), 855–66.

Black, L., Neel, J., & Benson, G. (2008, August). NCTAF/GSU Induction Project, Final Report, Georgia State University.

Bowlby, J. (1951). *Maternal care and mental health* [monograph]. World Health Organization.

Campos, J. J., Langer, A., & Krowitz, A. (1970). Cardiac responses on the visual cliff in prelocomotor human infants. *Science, 170*(3954), 196–97.

Chambers, R., Chuen Yee Lo, B., & Allen, N. B. (2008). The impact of intensive mindfulness training on attentional control, cognitive style, and affect. *Cog Ther Res 32*, 303–22.

Condon, P., Desbordes, G., Miller, W., & Desterno, D. (2013). Meditation increases compassionate responses to suffering. *Psychological Science*, doi:10.1177/0956797613485603

Davidson, R. J., Kabat-Zinn, J., Schumacher, J., Rozenkrantz, M., Muller, D., & Santorelli, S. F. (2003). Alterations in the brain and immune function produced by mindfulness meditation. *Psychomet Med, 65*, 564–70. doi:10.1097/01.PSY.0000077505.67574.E3

Diaz, F. (2013, Aug 1). Mindfulness, attention, and flow during music listening: An empirical investigation. *Int J Music Ed, 31*, 310–20.

Durlak, J., Weissberg, R., Dymnicki, A., Taylor, R., & Schellinger, K. (2011). The impact of enhancing students' social and emotional learning: A meta-analysis of school-based universal interventions. *Child Devel, 82*(1), 405–32.

Emanuel, E. (2012, June 23). Share the wealth. *New York Times*.

Emerson, D. (2011). *Overcoming trauma through yoga.* Berkeley, CA: North Atlantic Books.

Felitti, V. J., Anda, R. F., Nordenberg, D., Williamson, D. F., Spitz, A. M., Edwards, V., . . . & Marks, J. S. (1998). Relationship of childhood abuse and household dysfunction to many of the leading causes of death in adults: The adverse childhood experiences (ACE) study. *Am Jo Prevent Med, 14*(4), 245–58.

Gardner, H. (1983). *Frames of mind: The theory of multiple intelligences.* New York, NY: Basic Books.

Gopnik, A., Meltzoff, A., Kuhl, P. (2000). *The scientist in the crib.* New York, NY: Perennial.

Hölzel, B. K., Carmody, J., Vangel, M., Congleton, C., Yerramsetti, S. M., Gard, T., & Lazar, S. W. (2011). Mindfulness practice leads to increases in regional brain gray matter density. *Psychiatr Res: Neuroimag, 191*(1), 36. doi: 10.1016/j.pscychresns.2010.08.006

Jacobs, T. L., Epel, E. S., Lin, J., Blackburn, E. H., Wolkowitz, O. M., Bridwell, D. A., & Saron, C. D. (2011). Intensive meditation training, immune cell telomerase activity, and psychological mediators. *Psychoneuroendocrinology 36*(5), 664–81. doi: 10.1016/j.psyneuen.2010.09.010

Jha, A. P., Krompinger, J., & Baime, M. J. (2007). Mindfulness training modifies subsystems of attention. *Cog Affect Behav Neurosci 7*, 109–19.

Kabat-Zinn, J., Lipworth, L., Burrey, R., & Sellers, W. (1986). Four-year follow up of a meditation-based program for the self-regulation of pain. *Clinical Joint Pain, 2*, 159–173.

Kabat-Zinn, J. (1982). An out-patient program in behavioral medicine for chronic pain patients based on the practice of mindfulness meditation. *General Hospital Psychiatry, 4*, 33.47.

Kabat-Zinn, J., Lipworth, L., & Burrey, R. (1995). The clinical use of mindfulness meditation for the self-regulation of chronic pain. *Journal of Behavioral Medicine, 8*, 163–190.

Kemeny, M., Foltz, C., Cavanagh, J., Cullen, M., Giese-Davis, J., Rosenberg, E., . . . & Ekman, P. (2012). Contemplative/emotion training reduces negative emotional behavior and promotes prosocial responses, emotion. *Am Psychol Assoc, 12*(2), 338–50.

Kuyken, W., Byford, S., Taylor, R. S., Watkins, E., Holden, E., White, K., . . . & Teasdale, J. D. (2008). Mindfulness-based cognitive therapy to prevent relapse in recurrent depression. *J Consult Clin Psychol, 76*(6), 966–78. doi: 10.1037/a0013786

Levine, P. (1997). *Waking the tiger.* Berkeley, CA: North Atlantic Books.

Maughan, A., & Cicchetti, D. (2002). Impact of child maltreatment and interadult violence on children's emotion regulation abilities and socioemotional adjustment. *Child Devel 73*(5), 1525–42.

Merikangas, K. R., He, J. P., Burstein, M., Swanson, S. A., Avenevoli, S., Cui, L., Benjet, C., . . . & Swendsen, J. (2010, October). Lifetime prevalence of mental disorders in U.S. adolescents: Results from the National Comorbidity Survey Replication—Adolescent Supplement (NCS-A). *J Am Acad Child Adolesc Psychiatry 49*(10), 980–89. doi: 10.1016/j.jaac.2010.05.017.

Mindful Research Guide. (2013). *Research publications on mindfulness, 1980–2012.* Retrieved August 2013 from http://www.mindful experience.org/mindfo.php.

Mrazek, M., Franklin, M., Tarchin Phillips, D., Baird, B., & Schooler, J. (2013, May). Mindfulness training improves working memory capacity and GRE performance while reducing mind wandering. *Psychol Sci, 24*(5), 776–81.

Napoli, M., Krech, P. R., Holley, L. C. (2005). Mindfulness training for elementary school students. *J Appl School Psychol, 21*(1), 99–125.

National Scientific Council on the Developing Child. (2012). *The science of neglect: The persistent absence of responsive care disrupts the developing brain.* Working Paper 12. Retrieved from http://www.developingchild.harvard.edu

Nerurkar, A., Yeh, G., Davis, R., Birdee, G., & Phillips, R. (2011). When conventional medical providers recommend unconventional medicine: Results of a national study. *Arch Intern Med, 171*(9), 862–64. doi:10.1001/archinternmed.2011.160

Northeastern University College of Science. (2013, April 1). Can meditation make you a more compassionate person? *ScienceDaily*. Retrieved September 6, 2013 from http://www.sciencedaily.com/releases/2013/04/130401111553.htm

O'Connor, T. G., Rutter, M., Beckett, C., Keaveney, L., & Kreppner, J. M. (2000). The effects of global severe privation on cognitive competence: Extension and longitudinal follow-up. *Child Development, 71*(2), 376–90.

Raes, F., Griffith, J., Van der Gucht, K., & Williams, M. (2013, Mar). School-based prevention and reduction of depression in adolescents: A cluster-randomized controlled trial of a mindfulness group program. *Mindfulness J*. doi: 10.1007/s12671-013-0202-1

Reardon, F. (2013, April 27). No rich child left behind. *New York Times*.

Rosch, P. (1997). Measuring job stress: Some comments on potential pitfalls. *Am J Health Prom, 11*(6), 400–401.

Salmon, P., Sephton, S., Weissbecke, I., Hoover, K., Ulmer, C., & Studts, J. I. (2004). Mindfulness meditation in clinical practice. *Cogn Behav Prac, 11*, 434–46.

Sibinga, E., Kerrigan, D., Stewart, M., Johnson, K., Magyari, T., & Ellen, J. (2011). Mindfulness instruction for urban youth. *J Altern Complement Med, 17*, 1–6.

Siegel, D., & Bryson, T. P. (2011). *The whole-brain child*. New York, NY: Random House.

Tang, Y., Yang, L., Leve, L., & Harold, G. (2012, Dec). Improving executive function and its neurobiological mechanisms through a mindfulness-based intervention: Advances within the field of developmental neuroscience. *Child Devel Persp 6*(4), 361–66.

Treleaven, D. (2012). *Meditation and trauma: A hermeneutic study of Western vipassana practice through the perspective of somatic experiencing* [dissertation]. California Institute of Integral Studies.

van der Kolk, B. A. (1994). The body keeps the score: Memory and the evolving psychobiology of post traumatic stress disorder. *Harv Rev Psychiatr, 1*(5).

Wahlstrom, K. (2002). Changing times: Findings from the first longitudinal study of later high school start times. *NASSP Bull 86*(633), 3–21.

Zeidan, F., Johnson, S. K., Diamond, B. J., David, Z., & Goolkasian, P. (2010). Mindfulness meditation improves cognition: Evidence of brief mental training. *Conscious Cog, 19*(2), 597–605.

Further Reading

Gina Biegal, *The Stress Reduction Workbook for Teens,* Instant Help, 2010.

Louis Cozolino, *The Social Neuroscience of Education*, W. W. Norton and Company, 2013.

Daniel Goleman, *Emotional Intelligence: 10th Anniversary Edition*, Bantam, 2006.

Thich Naht Hahn, *Planting Seeds*, Parallax Press, 2011.

Jennifer Cohen Harper, *Little Flower Yoga for Kids*, New Harbinger, 2013.

Judith Horstman, *Burlington Manual: Mindfulness in Public Schools*, Compiled by the South Burlington, Vermont, School District, 2013.

Jon Kabat-Zinn, *Full Catastrophe Living*, Random House, 2013.

Jon Kabat-Zinn, *Mindfulness for Beginners*, Sounds True, 2011.

Jon and Myla Kabat-Zinn, *Everyday Blessings*, Hyperion, 1998.

Susan Kaiser-Greenland, *The Mindful Child*, Atria Books, 2010.

Alfie Kohn, *Unconditional Parenting*, Atria Books, 2005.

Linda Lantieri and Daniel Goleman, *Building Emotional Intelligence*, Sounds True, 2008.

Richard Louv, *Last Child in the Woods*, Algonquin Books, 2008.

Kristen Neff, *Self-Compassion*, William Morrow, 2011.

Marshal Rosenberg, *Life-Enriching Education*, Puddle Dancer, 2003.

Tim Ryan, *A Mindful Nation*, Hay House, 2012.

Daniel Siegel and Tina Payne Bryson, *The Whole-Brain Child*, Delacorte Press, 2011.

Shauna Shapiro, *Mindful Discipline*, New Harbinger Press, 2014.

INDEX